Country Classics

COUNTRY CLASSICS

AUTHENTIC PROJECTS
YOU CAN BUILD
IN ONE WEEKEND

JOHN A. NELSON

Stackpole Books

Copyright © 1989 by Stackpole Books

Published by
STACKPOLE BOOKS
Cameron and Kelker Streets
P.O. Box 1831
Harrisburg, PA 17105

Printed in the United States of America

10 9 8 7 6 5 4 3 2 1

Library of Congress Cataloging-in-Publication Data

Nelson, John A., 1935–
    Country classics : authentic projects
you can build in one weekend / John A. Nelson
        p.   cm.
        ISBN 0-8117-0429-7
        ISBN 0-8117-2277-5 (pbk.)
        1. Furniture making 2. Country furniture—United States.
I. Title.
TT194.N45   1989
749.214—dc19
                                                                    88-20027
                                                                         CIP
                                                                         Rev

CONTENTS

Preface 5

Early Furniture and Accessories 7

Selecting Materials 9

Making the Projects 11

Hardware 17

Finishing and Staining 21

How to Use the Drawings 25

The Projects

Treenware 28

Footstools and Benches 58

Desk Boxes 70

Candle Boxes 97

Wall Boxes 118

Mirror 163

Pipe Boxes 166

Hanging Wall Shelves 184

Table 211

Blanket Chest 214

Appendices

Suppliers 217

Related Publications 219

Woodworking Associations, Clubs, and Guilds 219

For Further Study 220

To the four Js in my life: Joyce, my wife, and my three daughters, Julie, Joy, and Jennifer

PREFACE

This book will guide woodworkers in reproducing authentic-looking copies of primitive, colonial, and early American pieces. But more important, it provides an accurate record of those wonderfully unusual and unique small objects that were so important to the Americans who used them long ago.

Each project in this book is an exact copy of an authentic antique found throughout New England and the northeastern section of this country—right down to the sometimes unusual construction techniques used. No attempt has been made to improve upon the original construction methods even by using tools or methods available today. Whenever known, the kind of wood that was used on the original piece is indicated. If the original piece was painted, its original color and details are also given in as much detail as possible in order that the copy be as close to the original as possible. The chapter on finishing and staining explains how to apply a finish that will look like the 150-year-old original.

Every project reproduces a one-of-a-kind antique, probably made by hand and in many cases by a not-so-skilled craftsperson. Each was made to serve a particular, important need in days past. Today that need has probably changed or become obsolete, but the projects can still be functional for today's living.

All projects throughout this book have been carefully chosen so that only basic woodworking tools are necessary: The craftsperson with very limited space or only basic woodworking tools can make any of them. A lathe is not necessary except to make a few drawer pulls or wooden knobs. If you don't wish to make them, however, you may buy wooden knobs and drawer pulls very close to the original style from one of the many supply houses listed at the end of this book.

This room, from a family dwelling in the Shaker community (1818–1840) of New Lebanon, New York, demonstrates the simple, utilitarian beauty of early American furniture. *(Courtesy of H. Richard Dietrich, Jr., the Philadelphia Museum of Art.)*

Because each reader is at a different skill level and will have different tools, only very brief and basic instructions are given on how to make each of these reproductions. All projects are simple and should be easy to make in a few hours or at least over a weekend. Before starting work on any project in this book, however, carefully study the drawings so that you fully understand how it is to be made and assembled. The exploded-view drawing provided with each project will illustrate the exact assembly.

I hope you will enjoy making and living with these early pieces and that this book of simple projects will provide you with a way to acquire an interesting, one-of-a-kind collection of early Americana that will add warmth to your home for generations to come. I also hope that by making some of these simple projects, beginning woodworkers will gain the confidence to attempt more advanced projects found in other books or woodworking magazines.

All photographs of the projects throughout this book are of new "antiques" and are *not* photographs of the originals. Each has been made to look as old as the original. The choice of pieces to be included has been mine alone. Any comments or criticism from those using this book will be most welcome.

Special appreciation and thanks go to my wife, Joyce, for making sense of my scribblings and notes and for typing them into something sensible. Thanks also to my good friends Jerry Ernce, who got me started in woodworking, and Bill Bigelow, for being my mentor and adviser throughout this book. Thanks, of course, to the many antique dealers, flea market merchants, and friends throughout New England who allowed me to study, measure, and photograph their wonderful, one-of-a-kind antiques. And I would especially like to thank Dennis A. Waters and his staff at the Oak Street Studio of Exeter, New Hampshire, and Deborah Porter of Hancock, New Hampshire, for the very fine photographs that captured each "antique" just right. Without the help of the above people, this book could not have been completed.

John A. Nelson
Peterborough, New Hampshire
1987

Early Furniture and Accessories

The early settlers brought with them little but tradition when they began settling the new land. They had to begin by building their own homes—and, of course, the furnishings they absolutely needed. Most early settlers had few and meager tools to work with; many had limited building skills. The homes and furnishings they produced were by necessity crude or "primitive"—a term that is applied to many of those early pieces today. This book contains many such primitives: It is a unique style well worth reproducing.

Material was one problem the early settlers didn't have. Wood was abundant: Early settlers worked with first-cut timber from fully matured forests. European craftsmen of that time must have been as envious of the settlers as we are today for the prime timber supply available to them. These trees had been growing for well over one hundred years. The wood was straight grained, tough, clear, and free from defects, reaching widths almost impossible to find today. Ironically, in those days narrow boards were more desired than wide because it was more difficult to rip wood to size. Older houses can be found with narrow floorboards in the living room and boards over 24 inches wide in the attic.

The lumber we use today is from forests that have been logged off three and four times since the first cutting. Our lumber is frequently full of knots and contains many more defects than the original trees. In New Hampshire it is not uncommon to find a beautiful stone fence running through an old stand of trees, indicating that the land had at one time been cleared for pasture on one or both sides of the fence.

In New Hampshire it is not uncommon to find a stone fence running through an old stand of trees, indicating that early settlers once cleared the land on one or both sides.

All pieces in those days were built to serve a particular function—design was not an important concern. Unlike today's trends in furniture, the idea that "form follows function" surely applied. Some early pieces were actually out of proportion and somewhat awkward, but their character is obvious. This book has many projects with a lot of character!

Furniture and accessories made during the British rule were called "colonial," and those made after our independence from England are referred to as "early American." These designs did not change overnight, but there was a gradual evolution from colonial to early American style.

In doing the research for this book, I thought each and every project would be quite different, but after measuring, drawing, and building them all, I found to my surprise that they are very much alike in size and type of construction. Except for superficial outer design shapes, they are assembled much the same way, are very close to the same overall sizes, and serve the same functions regardless of their geographical origin, be it northern New Hampshire or southern Rhode Island.

Because each piece had a particular purpose, a purpose probably obsolete today, you must be imaginative in finding a use for each piece without destroying the design. Today an early pipe box, once used to store long-stemmed clay pipes and tobacco, can be used as a convenient place to store candles and matches, or for outgoing mail with stamps stored in the drawer; the many wall boxes in this book make great planters. Whatever their contemporary use, the projects reflect the independent spirit of those who lived in the early days of our country—a spirit passed on today to those who follow them in making these pieces.

Selecting Materials

As lumber for these projects will probably be the most expensive material you will purchase, it is a good idea to know a little about your choices. All lumber is either hardwood or softwood. Hardwoods are deciduous, trees that lose their leaves in the fall, and softwoods are coniferous, or evergreen. A few hardwoods are softer than some softwoods, but on the whole, hardwoods are stronger and much more durable. Tougher to work, hardwood takes a finish and a stain beautifully. It usually costs more than softwood but is well worth the difference in price.

All wood contains pores, or open spaces. Wood like oak and mahogany has pores that are very noticeable and should probably be filled for a nice appearance. Wood like maple and birch has what is called a "closed grain" and lends itself to a beautiful, smooth finish.

The grain of the wood is formed by the pattern of growth of that particular tree. Each year the circumference of a tree is girdled with an annular ring, which forms a new and hard fibrous layer. The growth of most trees is regular and these annular rings are evenly spaced, but in other trees the growth is very uneven, creating irregular spacing and thickness. The pattern formed by the rings is the grain pattern we see when the tree is cut into lumber.

The softwoods used for most of the projects in this book are pine, spruce, and fir. Pine was the favorite wood for colonial settlers because it was the easiest to work, especially for simple accessories like those found in this book. Hardwoods most used were maple, walnut, oak, cherry, poplar, and birch.

Always buy dried lumber. Green lumber will shrink, twist, and warp while drying. Purchase the best lumber you can find for these projects: Your work will be much easier and the finished project much better. The cost difference between an inexpensive piece of wood and the best you can find will be very little, as none of these small projects require much material.

Lumber is sold by the "board foot." A board foot is a piece of wood that is 1 inch thick, 12 inches wide, and 12 inches long. The formula, *in inches*:

width × thickness × length ÷ 144 = board feet

So a piece of wood 4 inches wide, 2 inches thick, and 6 feet (72 inches) long contains 4 board feet of lumber:

4 × 2 × 72 = 576
576 ÷ 144 = 4 board feet

For a quick, easy method to calculate board feet, see Figure 1. Given a particular thickness and width, find the corresponding "factor" and multiply it by the length of the board *in feet*. So a board 1 inch thick, 5 inches wide, and 12 feet long contains 5.004 board feet of lumber:

12 × 0.417 = 5.004

FIGURE 1 BOARD FEET

To calculate the number of board feet in a piece of lumber, locate the correct factor for the lumber's width and thickness, then multiply that factor by the lumber's lineal length (in feet).

WIDTH (INCHES)	THICKNESS	
	½ INCH	1 INCH
2	.093	.167
3	.125	.250
4	.166	.333
5	.309	.417
6	.250	.500
8	.333	.666
10	.417	.833
12	.500	1.000

The term *lineal length* refers to the actual length of any board; dressed, or finished, lumber is smaller than its listed measurements because of the finishing process (see Figure 2).

A few projects call for wide boards, the best choice for authenticity. If you can't find them, glue narrow boards together to obtain the required width. Care should be given to matching grain patterns so that the joint will not be noticeable. Don't be concerned about strength, as a glued joint is as strong as a single piece of wood and probably will not warp.

FIGURE 2

ROUGH LUMBER IN INCHES	FINISHED LUMBER IN INCHES
1 × 2	$3/4 \times 1\,5/8$
1 × 3	$3/4 \times 2\,5/8$
1 × 4	$3/4 \times 3\,5/8$
1 × 5	$3/4 \times 4\,5/8$
1 × 6	$3/4 \times 5\,5/8$
1 × 8	$3/4 \times 7\,1/2$
1 × 10	$3/4 \times 9\,1/2$
1 × 12	$3/4 \times 11\,1/2$

Making the Projects

After studying the plans, start by carefully making each part. Take care to make the pieces exactly to the correct size and square (90 degrees) to one another. Sand each piece separately, taking care to keep all edges sharp—some will be rounded after assembly.

After all pieces have been made, dry fit them: that is, carefully put the project together to check for fit before final assembly. If anything needs refitting or is a poor fit, this is the time to correct it.

If the pieces all fit correctly, glue or nail the project together, again taking care that all fits are tight and square. If you are using hardwood, drill holes just smaller than the nail diameter to avoid splitting the wood when nailing.

Sand the project all over. It is at this time that the edges can be rounded if necessary, after which the project is ready for finishing.

IRREGULAR SHAPES

Many pieces featured here have curved or irregular shapes, which are illustrated on a grid. To draw these shapes full size, draw a grid on a sheet of paper or cardboard in the exact size indicated and carefully transfer the lines or points, square for square (see Figure 3).

If you use paper, transfer the shape to the wood with a piece of carbon paper. If cardboard is used, cut out the pattern and transfer it directly to the wood. If the pattern is symmetrical—that is, the same on each side of the center—simply draw and transfer half the pattern to the wood at a time—this will ensure that the design will be perfect on both sides of the center.

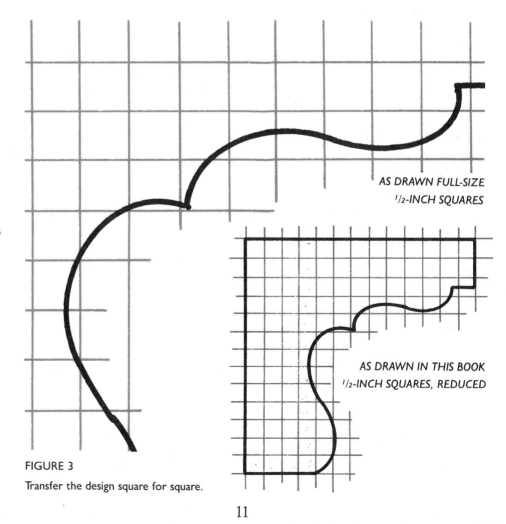

AS DRAWN FULL-SIZE
1/2-INCH SQUARES

AS DRAWN IN THIS BOOK
1/2-INCH SQUARES, REDUCED

FIGURE 3

Transfer the design square for square.

11

JOINTS

These projects use only four of the many kinds of joints available: the *butt joint*, the *rabbet joint*, the *dado joint*, and the *dovetail joint* (see Figure 4). They can be made by hand, without power tools, although the power tools will make the job easier.

Most projects in this book use the butt joint, the simplest of all joints. As its name implies, it is two boards that are butted up against each other and nailed together. The major disadvantage of the butt joint is that less wood is exposed for gluing or nailing. Also, nails sometimes back out of the joint over time, leaving an opening.

A rabbet joint is an L-shaped cut made along the edge of one board and overlapping the end of the other board. This joint is also nailed together, but the nails are hidden somewhat because they are put in from the sides. The front board of a drawer is a good example of a rabbet joint.

Dado joints are similar to rabbet joints except the cut leaves wood on both sides (see Figure 5). A drawer side is an excellent example of both a dado joint and a rabbet joint.

Dovetail joints were used on the sides of chests and drawers and on the tops of bureaus—they make a very tight joint and were usually used on better or more formal accessories (see Figure 6). Dovetailing was used in America starting around 1675. Early drawers used a dovetail joint for the front board and a dado joint for the back board, with one single, wide dovetail that was nailed in place. By 1730 drawers were made using three or four dovetails, and by 1800 and beyond dovetails had become very thin (see Figure 7).

FIGURE 4

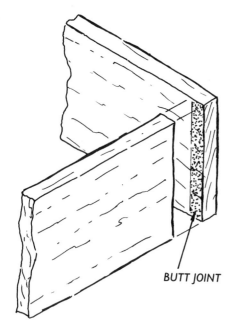

BUTT JOINT

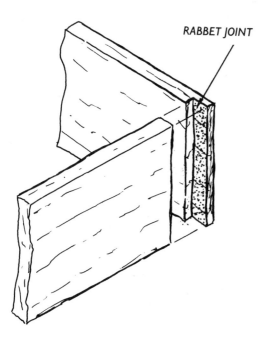

RABBET JOINT

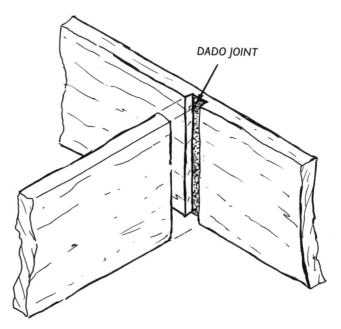

DADO JOINT

FIGURE 5

RABBET JOINT

SIDE OF DRAWER

The rabbet joint is shaped like an L;
the dado joint is a U.

DADO JOINT

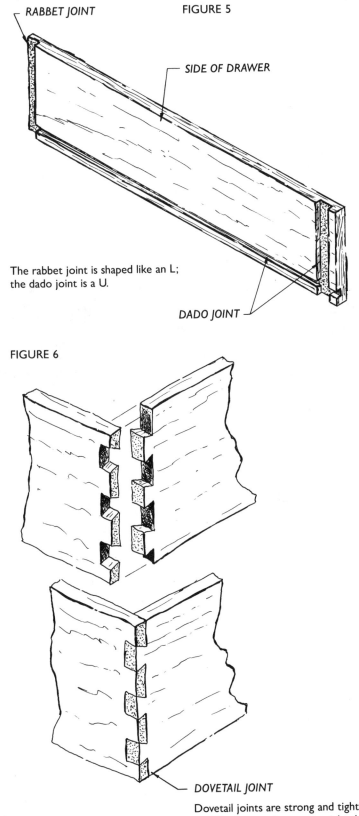

FIGURE 6

DOVETAIL JOINT

Dovetail joints are strong and tight . . . and not
as difficult to make as you might think.

FIGURE 7

SINGLE DOVETAIL

SCRIBE MARK

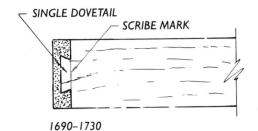

1690–1730

DRAWER SIDE

THICK

SCRIBE MARK

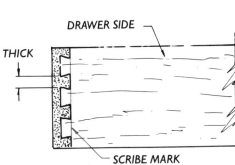

1730–1800

DRAWER FRONT

SCRIBE MARK

THIN

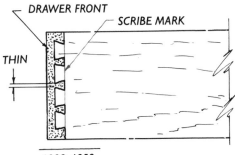

1800–1850

You can often tell the age of furniture from the
character of dovetail joints.

SHAPING

A few of the projects use molded edges or surfaces. These molded edges were probably done by hand with a special molding plane, a very satisfying method if you have the plane or can borrow one. Most of us do not have one at our disposal, however, so molded edges must be achieved by some other method. A scraper blade can be made by grinding a reverse profile into a piece of 1/16-inch-thick steel (see Figure 8) and used by scraping it into the wood, but perhaps the easiest method is to use a hand-held router. It is not very expensive and can make all the special edges required for the projects in this book.

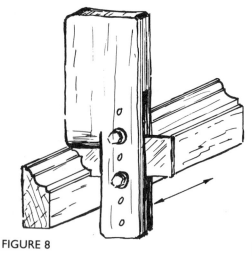

FIGURE 8

This handmade scraper blade will produce molded edges.

Crafters used this beader to create a decorative edge.

The router, perhaps the only power tool necessary for the projects in this book, can be used to make special edges. *(Courtesy of the Porter-Cable Corporation.)*

WORMHOLES

Some old pieces of furniture and accessories were attacked by insects that made what we call wormholes. The worms especially liked maple, walnut, oak, and most fruitwood, as well as pine and poplar. Wormholes appeared on the surface of the wood as small dots about the size of a pinhead. These holes can be faked using an ice pick or similar object.

A more obvious way to achieve wormholes is to use wood that has already been attacked by worms. (Wood with wormholes should be a good buy at the local lumberyard.) Because worms meander through wood, leaving channels going in all directions, wormy wood that has been sawed, planed or turned will show the side section of the wormholes, not the end or entrance. This is not authentic, but it does add that very old effect.

SCRIBE MARKS

Crafters of yesterday did not have pencils to mark off their work as we do today. Instead they used tools with sharp points to actually scratch, or "scribe," shallow grooves into the wood. These scribe marks can be seen on genuine antiques around dovetails, mortise joints, and in some cases, chair legs. To achieve that authentic look, you should consider using an awl or similar tool in place of a pencil to mark off your work. Leave the scribe marks on your finished project—they will add a lot to it and will indicate that it was handmade (see Figure 7).

Early crafters used sharp, pointed tools instead of pencils to mark off, or "scribe," their work.

GLUING

Glue was not in general use until after 1750, so many of the originals of the projects featured in this book were simply nailed or pinned together. If, by chance, any were glued, they were probably joined with "hot" animal hide glue. Because very good glue is available today, it is advisable that your reproductions be glued as well as nailed.

Wood glues are either hot or cold, depending on whether heat is used to prepare them. Hot glue, made from animal parts, is very strong and quick setting. Until just a few years ago, hot glue was considered the only truly satisfactory kind of glue to use in cabinetmaking. Recent developments in new and better cold glues have made such generalizations debatable. Cold glues are synthetics and vary in durability and strength. Some are slow in setting, others fast. For the projects in this book cold yellow glue is recommended. In using cold glue, follow instructions given on the label.

Always take care to clean excess glue from around the joint. If you wait five to ten minutes, just until the glue is almost set, you can remove most of it with a chisel. Do not use a wet cloth; it will weaken the glue in the joint and the water will close the grain of the wood, making it harder to stain. For the few projects that are a little difficult to hold together while gluing, there is a new hot glue made not from animal hides but of glue sticks that are inserted into a glue gun, heated, and then pushed through the tip. This glue dries very quickly and sets in about ten seconds without clamping.

DRAWER CONSTRUCTION

The drawer is easy to make. Think of it as a box without a top. Almost all drawers are made basically the same way, with a front, two sides, a bottom, and a back. All but two projects in this book use a simple kind of drawer that is called a "flush" drawer, which fits perfectly into the opening. The front piece does not overhang. Two or three projects use a drawer that has an overlapping drawer front. Both are easy to make, but the latter hides any imperfections in drawer construction or errors in size (see Figure 9).

To determine the size of the drawer, carefully measure the opening into which the drawer will fit. Record the height, width, and depth of the opening. Make the drawer about 1/32 to 1/16 inch less than the recorded height and about 1/16 to 3/32 inch less than the recorded width. The depth of the drawer should be about 1/16 inch shorter than the recorded depth.

Choose the wood for the drawer front carefully, as it should match the rest of the project. Try to find a piece of wood with an interesting grain pattern. The front piece should be thicker than the sides, back, and bottom, which are made of much thinner material and of secondary wood, such as pine or poplar.

Old drawer bottoms were usually chamfered (beveled) and set into grooves in the side and front boards of the drawer (see Figure 10). Do not glue the bottom board in place: Use two small nails, driven up from below and near the center of the bottom board.

As the drawer for each project will be slightly different, study Figures 11 and 12 before starting construction. Remember, original bottom boards had tapered sides.

Many drawers made after 1720 had handmade dovetail joints. These joints look difficult to make but are actually fairly easy and fun to do. There are many excellent books and magazines that illustrate how to make a dovetail joint.

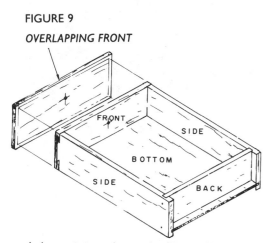

FIGURE 9

OVERLAPPING FRONT

FRONT · SIDE · BOTTOM · SIDE · BACK

A drawer is just a box without a top. The overlapping front is simply glued in place.

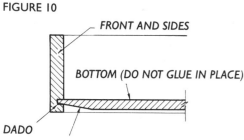

FIGURE 10

FRONT AND SIDES

BOTTOM (DO NOT GLUE IN PLACE)

DADO

TAPER (APPROXIMATELY 10 DEGREES)

The tapered edges of the bottom fit into the dado cuts of the front and sides.

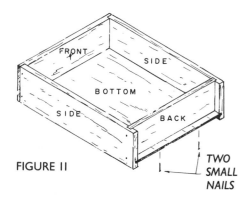

FRONT · SIDE · BOTTOM · SIDE · BACK

FIGURE 11

TWO SMALL NAILS

For authenticity, do not use glue. Instead, secure the bottom by driving two small nails through the bottom into the back. Shown is a flush drawer.

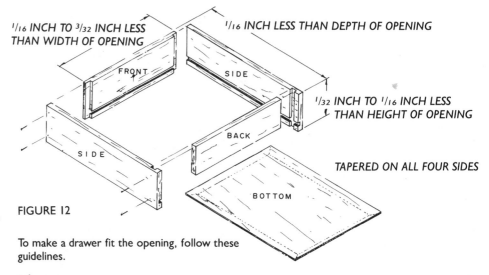

1/16 INCH TO 3/32 INCH LESS THAN WIDTH OF OPENING

1/16 INCH LESS THAN DEPTH OF OPENING

FRONT · SIDE

1/32 INCH TO 1/16 INCH LESS THAN HEIGHT OF OPENING

SIDE · BACK

TAPERED ON ALL FOUR SIDES

BOTTOM

FIGURE 12

To make a drawer fit the opening, follow these guidelines.

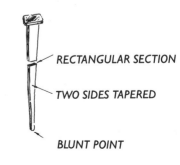

Hardware

As with lumber, the extra money spent on high-quality, authentic hardware adds little to the overall cost of the project and is well worth the difference. At the end of this book is a list of quality vendors that sell such hardware; flea markets are another good place to look. An old, authentic hinge, though rusty and worn, will add a lot of character to your project and will really make it look original.

PINS

Because nails were so expensive, wooden pins were sometimes used in their place, especially in mortise and tenon joints. Early pins were referred to as "trunnels." Some were tapered, but contrary to popular belief, none were round in cross section. Rather they were polygonal or even square, made that way so that the edges of the pin would bite into the round hole into which they were driven, securing them tightly. If you use pins on any projects in this book, take care not to use round, dowel-like pins. Leave the ends projecting from the surface 1/16 inch or more to simulate old age, and drill the holes for the pins at a slight angle to improve holding power (see Figure 13).

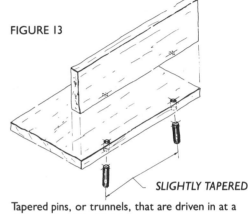

FIGURE 13

SLIGHTLY TAPERED

Tapered pins, or trunnels, that are driven in at a slight angle will hold tightly.

NAILS

Nails were used to hold parts of early country accessories in place. Glue would not have been used on such simple objects as those found in this book. From the seventeenth century probably through to the nineteenth century, nails were hand forged from pure iron. They were rust-resistant and bent very easily but seldom broke. Early hand-forged nails were square in cross section and tapered on all four sides to a point (see Figure 14). Hand-forged nails range in size from tiny brads, used to apply moldings, to large common nails, used for construction of buildings and bridges. Early nails had bumpy "rose" heads, square heads, or sometimes no heads at all. Because they were hand forged, one at a time, no two nails were made exactly alike.

Machine-cut square nails, somewhat resembling original hand-forged nails, were made from 1790 to 1870 or so. They are rectangular in cross section and tapered on two opposite sides (see Figure 14). Machine-cut nails made in large quantities after 1815 had blunt, squared-off points and tended to rust.

Today, machine-cut nails can be purchased from several suppliers for very reasonable prices; see the list at the back of this book. It is recommended that these nails be used in building the projects to give your work an authentic look and feel, but you can safely use "modern" (c. 1870) roundhead steel wire nails as well. After the project is completed, they will not be seen—only you will know.

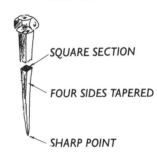

FIGURE 14

SQUARE SECTION

FOUR SIDES TAPERED

SHARP POINT

HANDMADE NAIL

RECTANGULAR SECTION

TWO SIDES TAPERED

BLUNT POINT

MACHINE-MADE NAIL

FIGURE 15

HANDMADE SCREW

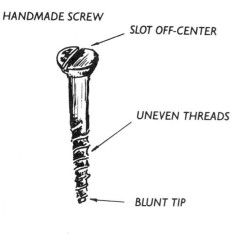

SLOT OFF-CENTER

UNEVEN THREADS

BLUNT TIP

SCREWS

Screws were used as early as 1700. Like nails, the first screws were made by hand but were much more expensive to produce than nails, so they were not used nearly as much—especially in primitive or early country accessories, such as those in this book.

Early screws were only 1/2 inch in length or shorter. Their threads were made by hand and were uneven, wide, and rounded on the edges. The tips of the threads were blunt, and the heads flat. The slot was narrow, shallow, and often off center. See Figure 15.

Machine-cut screws were invented around 1815. The first screws were somewhat like the handmade screws but tended to be longer. By 1850 machine-cut screws were exactly like those of today.

FIGURE 16

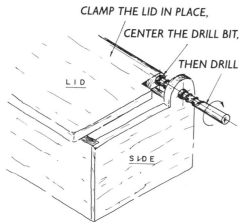

CLAMP THE LID IN PLACE,

CENTER THE DRILL BIT,

THEN DRILL

LID

SIDE

Drilling the hole for the dowel with the lid in place will give a good fit.

HINGES

Wood dowel hinge

Four projects in this book use wooden hinges to support the lids. A wood dowel hinge is made by extending the sides of the box above the lid, drilling a hole through the sides into the lid, and inserting two wood dowels (or nails) through the holes (see Figure 16). These hinges are simple to make and give the impression of being very old. Take care, however, to drill the hole into the lid after the holes in the sides have been drilled. A good way of ensuring a perfect fit is to clamp or secure the lid in place, exactly as it is to be when closed, and drill the holes into the lid through the holes in the side pieces, as illustrated. Add the wood dowels last.

FIGURE 17

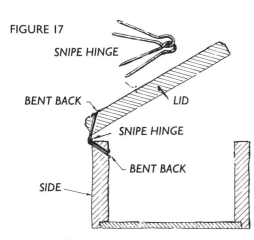

SNIPE HINGE

BENT BACK

LID

SNIPE HINGE

BENT BACK

SIDE

This section view of a lidded box shows how a snipe hinge works. Bend the points back and drive them into the wood.

Snipe hinge

Another old type of hinge is the "snipe" hinge, sometimes referred to as a staple hinge, clinch hinge, or cotterpin hinge. One of the earliest hinges, it is like two hairpins joined together (see Figure 17).

Snipe hinges were hand forged from two iron rods that ranged from 1/16 inch to 3/32 inch thick with pointed ends. The sharp pointed ends were inserted into holes in furniture at an angle, with the points poking through the other side (see Figure 17). The protruding points were spread apart and "clinched," or bent back around and driven into the other side of the wood. These hinges wore out very quickly. It is not uncommon to find early pieces that have modern hinges alongside the original snipe hinges.

Snipe hinges were used mostly on chest lids and sometimes on cupboard doors from 1719 to 1800.

Butterfly hinge

These hinges were used from 1700 to around 1765. They were called butterfly hinges because of their splayed sides (see Figure 18). Hand-forged hinges were thicker through the center section and thinner at the edges. They were attached with handmade screws or rosehead nails. The nails were usually clinched back through the wood from behind.

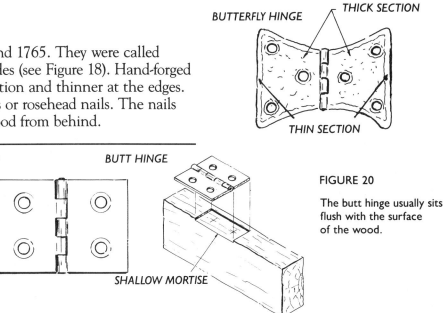

FIGURE 18

BUTTERFLY HINGE — THICK SECTION

THIN SECTION

Butt hinge

Butt hinges, easily identified by their square ends, were used as early as 1815 (see Figure 19). They are usually set into shallow mortises in the wood, so the hinge is flush with the surface (see Figure 20).

FIGURE 19   **BUTT HINGE**

SHALLOW MORTISE

FIGURE 20

The butt hinge usually sits flush with the surface of the wood.

KNOBS

Wooden knobs, originally referred to as "thumb-pulls," were probably the first kind of knob used on early American country accessories and furniture. They were almost always made of hardwood and were sometimes of a different wood than the piece itself.

A few projects in this book call for metal knobs. Usually brass, these tended to be more formal in design than wooden knobs. Brass knobs made their appearance in America around 1675 and were cast brass.

Original brass knobs were meant to be highly polished. Through the years, however, people came to believe that old brasses should be left tarnished. Today many inexpensive reproductions are made to look tarnished, which is incorrect. Original polished brass was also very light in color. It was not until after 1755 that more copper was added to the brass, which tended to make it darker, as it is today.

Original wooden knobs were generally longer than they were wide and ranged from 1 inch to 2 inches in length (see Figure 21). Some knobs were driven into a hole of a smaller diameter than the knob shank (see Figure 22). Others were held in place by a wooden peg driven through a small hole in the shank (see Figure 23), which is what is used for most of the projects in this book. Sometime after 1825, as screws became more available, hardwood knobs were held in place by screws inserted from behind (see Figure 24).

Later, wooden knobs tended to be wider than they were long. Called mushroom knobs, they were fastened using the same methods as the early knobs. Figure 25 offers some designs to copy if you have a lathe.

FIGURE 21

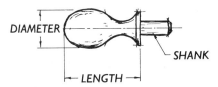

DIAMETER — SHANK

LENGTH

Early knobs were usually longer than their diameters.

FIGURE 22

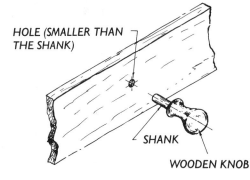

HOLE (SMALLER THAN THE SHANK)

SHANK

WOODEN KNOB

So that a wooden knob fits tightly, drill the hole slightly smaller than the diameter of the shank.

FIGURE 23

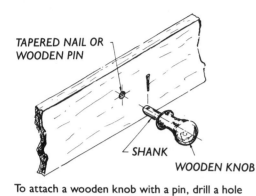

TAPERED NAIL OR WOODEN PIN

SHANK

WOODEN KNOB

To attach a wooden knob with a pin, drill a hole in the shank x inches along the shank, where x equals the thickness of the drawer front plus half the diameter of the pin.

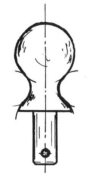

"X"

FIGURE 24

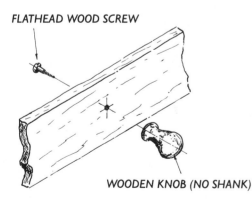

FLATHEAD WOOD SCREW

WOODEN KNOB (NO SHANK)

This hardwood knob is attached to the drawer with a screw.

If you are going to use modern purchased knobs, you can make them look older by drilling a hole into each and gluing a dowel into the hole (see Figure 26).

FIGURE 25

EARLY KNOBS

LATER KNOBS

The later knobs are nearly as fat as they are long.

FIGURE 26

¼-INCH DOWEL

¼-INCH HOLE

PURCHASED KNOB

HOLE FOR PIN

CHAMFERED END

DOWEL, GLUED IN PLACE

To make a modern wooden knob look more authentic, drill a hole and glue a dowel in place, as a substitute for a shank. Secure the knob to the drawer front with a tapered nail or wooden pin.

Finishing and Staining

After completing construction, you will be ready to finish your project. This is the important part and should not be rushed. Remember, the finish will be seen for years to come. No matter how good the wood and hardware and no matter how tight the joints, a poor finish will ruin your project.

PREPARING

Step 1. All joints should be checked for tight fits. If necessary, apply water putty to them and allow ample time for them to dry. For the projects found in this book it will probably not be necessary to set and fill nailheads; they are generally left showing. If you do not want to see the nailheads, however, set and water-putty them now.

Step 2. Sand the project all over in the direction of the grain. If sanding is done by hand, use a sanding block and keep all corners sharp until Step 3. Use an 80-grit paper first, then resand all over using a 120-grit paper and, if necessary, again using a 180-grit paper.

Step 3. If you want any of the edges slightly rounded, now is the time to do so. First, carefully study the object and try to imagine how it would have been used through the years. Then, using a rasp, judiciously round the edges where you think wear would have occurred. Finally, sand the entire project and the new "worn" edges with 120-grit paper, then with 180-grit paper.

Step 4. Distressing will help make these copies of 150-year-old antiques look old. It can be done many ways. Roll a piece of coral stone about 3 inches in diameter, or a similar object, across the various surfaces. Don't be afraid to add a few scratches at random here and there, especially on the bottoms or backs, where an object would have been worn the most.

Step 5. Carefully check that all surfaces are smooth, dry, and dust-free, especially if softwood is used.

A palm grip sander is useful in completing these projects, but they can also be sanded by hand. *(Courtesy of the Porter-Cable Corporation.)*

A 3-inch coral stone or similar object is rolled across the surface of the wood for distress marks, which help make the piece look old.

FILLERS

A paste filler should be used for porous wood, such as oak or mahogany. Purchase paste filler slightly darker than the color of your wood, which will turn darker with age. Before using paste filler, thin it with turpentine so that it can be brushed on. Use a stiff brush and brush with the grain to fill the pores. In fifteen or twenty minutes, wipe off the filler across the grain with a piece of burlap, taking care to leave filler in the pores. Apply a second coat if necessary and let dry for twenty-four hours.

STAINING

The two major kinds of stain are water stain and oil stain. Water stains are purchased in powder form and mixed as needed by dissolving the powder in hot water. They have a tendency to raise the grain of the wood. If a water stain is used, the surface should be lightly sanded with fine paper after it dries. Oil stains are made from pigments ground in linseed oil; they do not raise the grain. You'll want to follow the instructions given on the container, whichever kind of stain you use, but here is the basic procedure.

Step 1. Test the stain on a scrap piece of the lumber you're using to make certain it will be the color you want.

Step 2. Wipe or brush on the stain as quickly and as evenly as possible to avoid overlapping streaks. If a darker finish is desired, apply more than one coat of stain. Try not to apply too much stain on the end grain, as it will darken much more. Allow the piece to dry in a dust-free area for at least twenty-four hours.

FINISHES

Shellac provides a hard surface, is easy to apply, and dries in a few hours. For best results, thin slightly with alcohol and apply three or four light coats. Several coats of thin shellac are much better than one or two thick coats. Sand lightly with extra-fine paper between coats, but be sure afterward to rub the entire surface with a dampened cloth to remove any dust. For that antique effect, strive for a smooth, satin finish, not a high-gloss coat.

Varnish is easy to brush on and dries to a smooth, hard finish within twenty-four hours. It makes an excellent transparent, deep-looking finish. Be sure to apply varnish in a completely dust-free area. Apply one or two coats directly from the can with long even strokes. Rub with 0000 steel wool between each coat and after the last coat. As with shellac, do not leave a glossy finish—an antique would not have a high gloss after 150 years.

Oil finishes are especially easy to use for projects like those in this book. They are easy to apply, long lasting, and improve wood permanently, and they never need resanding. Apply a heavy, wet coat uniformly to all surfaces and let it set for twenty or thirty minutes. Wipe dry or until you have a nice satin finish.

WASH COAT

Even with the distress marks and scratches, your project probably still looks new. To give your project a 150-year-old look, take a cloth and simply wipe on a coat of oil-base black paint directly from the can. Take care to get the black paint in all distress marks and scratches. Wipe off all paint immediately, before it dries, but leave the black paint in all the corners, joints, scratches, and distress marks. If you goof or don't like your work, simply wipe the paint off with turpentine on a cloth. This wash coat should make your project look like an original antique.

FOR THE LOOK OF OLD PAINT

Follow the first five steps outlined for preparing your project for finishing.

Step 6. Seal the wood with a light coat of 50 percent alcohol and 50 percent shellac. After it is dry, rub lightly with 0000 steel wool and wipe clean.

Step 7. Apply an even coat of paint, taking care to use an old color (see the suppliers' list at the end of the book for recommended paints). Let dry for forty-eight hours. Do not paint the backs or bottoms—in the originals, these parts were seldom painted.

Step 8. With 120-grit paper, sand all the rounded edges you made for "wear" marks in Step 4. If these edges were worn, the paint surely would have worn off also. Sand away paint from all sharp edges and corners; they, too, would wear through the years.

Step 9. Lightly sand all over with 180-grit paper to remove new paint gloss. Wipe clean.

Step 10. With a cloth, wipe on a coat of oil-base black paint directly from the can. Take care to get the black paint in all corners, distress marks, and scratches. Don't forget the unpainted back and bottom. Wipe the paint off immediately, before it dries, but leave it in all corners, joints, scratches, and distress marks. If you apply too much, wipe off with turpentine-dipped cloth. Let dry for twenty-four hours. Apply a light coat of paste wax.

FOR EXTRA AGING

For that extra-aged look, apply two coats of paint, each a different color, such as powder blue for the first coat and antique brick red for the second. Allow twenty-four hours between coats. After the second coat has dried for forty-eight hours or more, follow Steps 8 and 9, but sand through the top coat so that the first color shows through here and there at worn areas. Finish with Step 10. This technique is especially good on such projects as footstools or large painted wall boxes.

Extra aging can be simulated by applying two coats of paint, each a different color, and sanding the top coat at the worn areas so that the first color shows through.

FOR A CRINKLE FINISH

If you wish to give your painted project an aged, crinkle finish, follow these steps. After Step 6 in preparing your project, apply a coat of liquid hide glue over the surfaces to be painted. Let dry for twelve hours and then paint a coat of gesso over the glue. Paint lightly, and do not go over any strokes. In ten to fifteen seconds the gesso will start to crinkle. Let dry for twenty-four hours in a very dry area. After twenty-four hours or more, continue to Steps 7 through 10. (Experiment on scrap wood first.)

Visits to museums, antique shops, and flea markets will provide you with a realistic idea of what an antique should look like and what kind of finish will make your reproduction look 150 years old.

By achieving such a look, you will produce a project that appears to be authentic, and you may have fun fooling your friends into thinking it's an antique. However, should you decide to sell the piece, you'll want to avoid legal problems by making certain that potential buyers know it is a reproduction only.

SMOKE GRAINING

Smoke graining was a very crude process common folk used on pine to simulate the expensive walnut and mahogany wood that only aristocrats could afford. One project in this book, the whale shelf, uses this finishing technique, which is simple to do. (*Note:* You may want to practice this technique on a scrap of wood before attempting it on your project.)

Paint the piece whatever brown-base color you wish and let it dry twenty-four hours. Sand it smooth and apply a coat of varnish. Wait about two hours, or until the surface is tacky. Attach a *short*—2 inches or so—candle to a tuna fish can, which will catch the drippings.

If your project is small, hold the piece in one hand and move the candle underneath, using a sweeping motion. If the piece is large, however, you will have to hold it above the candle and, in effect, work upside down, also using the sweeping motion. Keep the piece 3 to 4 inches above the flame so that it doesn't blister.

For more smoke, hold a large nail or similar object in the flame, but be careful not to burn yourself in the process. Do not work in a draft.

Should you make a mistake during this process, let the varnish dry completely, then lightly sand the piece again, repaint with the base color, and start over. In the event that the varnish blisters, sand it down until it's smooth (don't strip off the base color), apply another coat of varnish, and when that coat is tacky, begin with the candle again.

After you achieve the desired effect, allow to dry for twenty-four hours. Taking care not to blur the smoking effect, apply a final coat of varnish using a bristle varnish brush (do not use a nylon brush).

Let dry twenty-four hours and sand lightly with a fine sandpaper. Wipe with a soft rag and add a coat of paste wax. Your reproduction is now ready for use for the next 150 years.

How to Use the Drawings

With each project there is a two-view drawing; one view is the *front view* and the other is either the *right view* or the *top view*. The views are positioned so that the front view is always the most important view and the starting place for studying the drawings. The right view is located directly to the right of the front view and the top view is located directly above the front view.

Dash lines indicate hidden surfaces or features within the object. Think of these lines as X rays showing what the inside will look like. Most drawer assemblies are shown with dash lines.

At times a *section view* is used to further illustrate a particular feature of the project. The section view is a partial view and illustrates only a portion of the project, such as a detail of a drawer construction.

Each project also has an *exploded view*, which illustrates the project as it is to be put together. Study the drawings until you fully understand how the project is to be assembled before you begin work.

The Projects

TREENWARE

The wooden objects presented in this book—called *treen*ware after the Anglo-Saxon plural for *tree*—once brought comfort to the homes of colonial housewives, who delighted in using them. In today's homes they add warmth and charm, as well as a pleasant reminder of life long ago. The originals are widely sought after and collected for their natural, unpretentious beauty and form.

The cutting boards, pie peel, picture frame, drying rack, dough box, and other such objects in this section are excellent examples of all kinds of early treenware.

Cutting Board Designs

Most cutting boards were made of maple, cherry, or almost any other hardwood. They were found throughout New England. Cutting boards should be made of one piece of wood and finished with a nontoxic finish. Sizes range from 7½ to 15 inches in diameter.

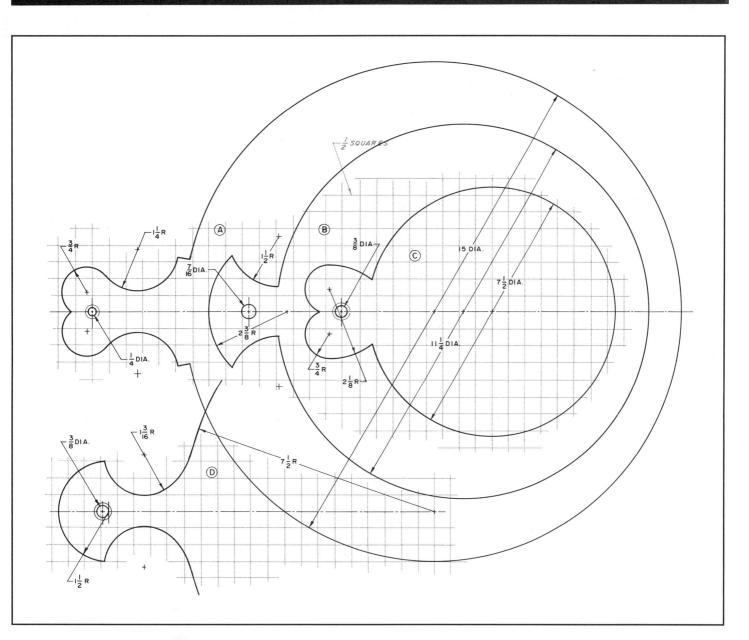

PROJECT	INCHES
A	3/4 × 15 × 19
B	3/4 × 11¼ × 12½
C	3/4 × 7½ × 9½
D	3/4 × SIZE TO SUIT

Pie Peel

In years past pie peels were used to lift bread, pies, and cakes out of the early brick ovens. This one is an example of a very early design, around 1700. The original was made of walnut and found in Sunapee, New Hampshire. To make the metal parts, cut the pieces out of a large tin can and heat them with a torch until they are blue. Let them cool and tack in place as shown. This pie peel measures 12 by 25 inches.

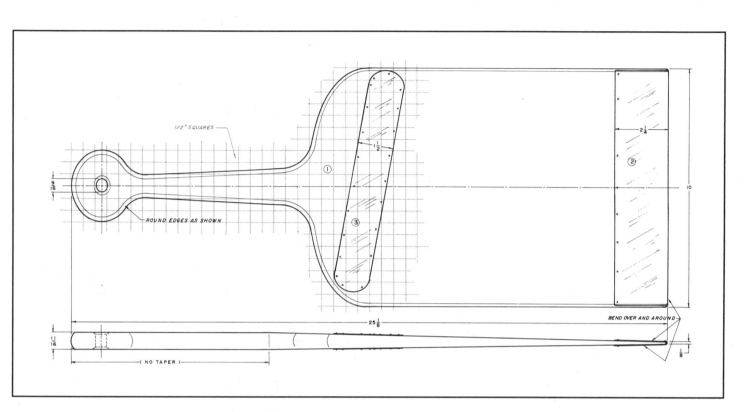

PART	INCHES	NEEDED
1 BODY	$^{11}/_{16} \times 10 \times 25^{1}/_{8}$	1
2 TIN TIP	$^{1}/_{32} \times 4^{5}/_{8} \times 9^{3}/_{4}$	1
3 TIN BRACE	$^{1}/_{32} \times 1^{1}/_{2} \times 9^{3}/_{8}$	2

Picture Frame

Early designs of picture frames like this one were rare. The exact date of this design is unknown. The original was made of pine and found in Sugarhill, New Hampshire. The frame measures 11 by 14 inches.

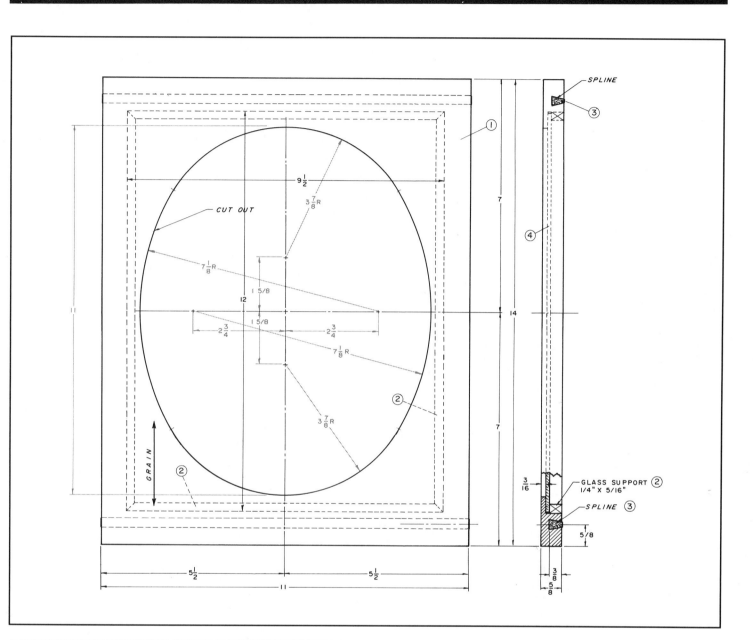

PART	INCHES	NEEDED
1 FRAME	$5/8 \times 11 \times 14$	1
2 GLASS SUPPORT	$1/4 \times 5/16 \times 44$	1
3 SPLINE	$1/4 \times 3/8 \times 11$	2
4 GLASS	$3/32 \times 9\,3/8 \times 11\,7/8$	1

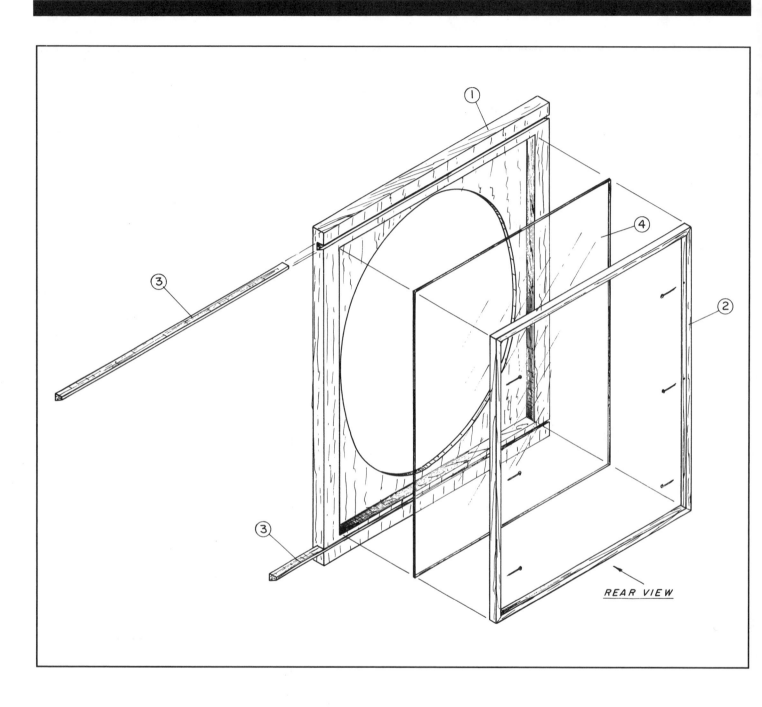

REAR VIEW

Clothes Hangers

These wonderful clothes hangers are copies from a Shaker design. They were usually made of hardwood and hang from twisted scraps of cloth.

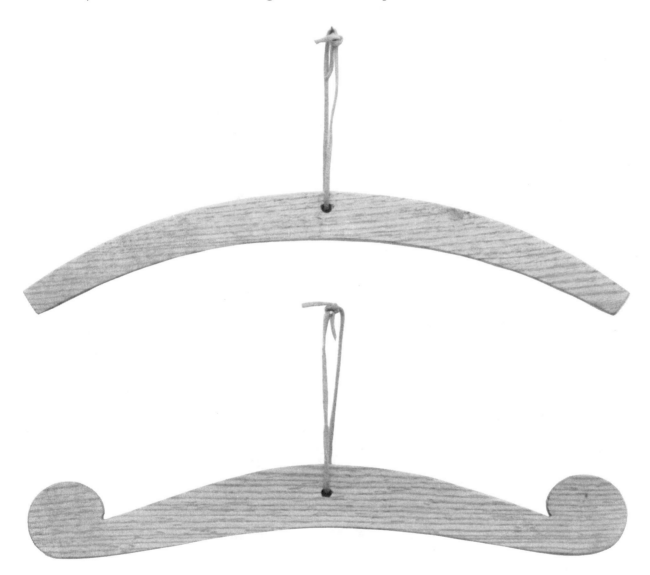

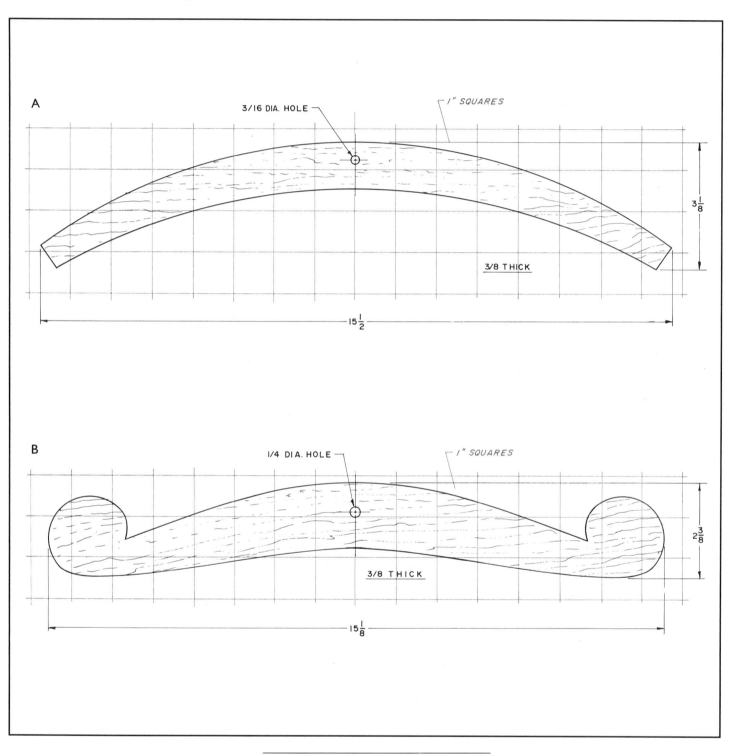

PROJECT	INCHES
A	$3/8 \times 3^{1}/8 \times 15^{1}/2$
B	$3/8 \times 2^{3}/8 \times 15^{1}/8$

Drying Rack

This very early style of drying rack (*c.* 1700) can still be functional today. Use it for drying clothes or displaying a favorite quilt. The original had mortise and tenon joints and was made of unfinished pine. Its origin is unknown. The rack measures 13 inches deep by 20 inches wide by 36 inches high.

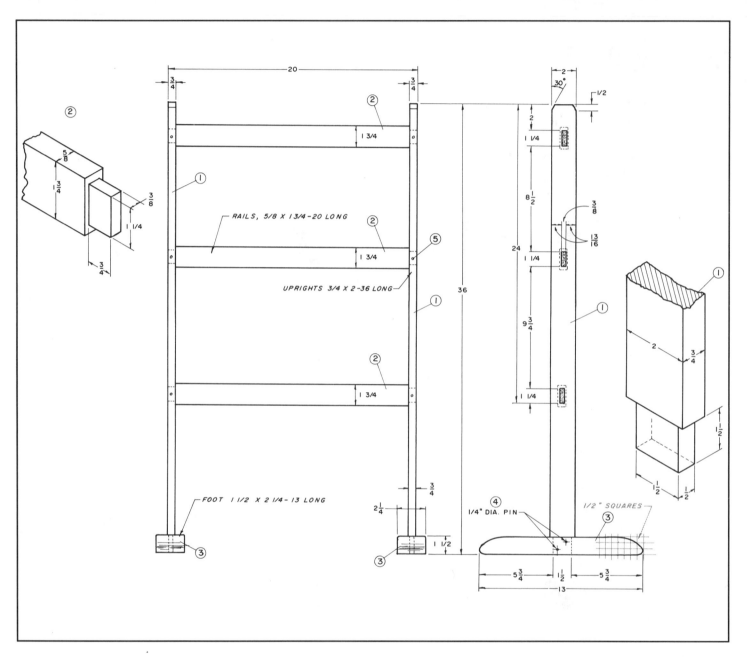

PART	INCHES	NEEDED
1 UPRIGHT	$3/4 \times 2 \times 36$	2
2 RAIL	$5/8 \times 1\,3/4 \times 20$	3
3 FOOT	$1\,1/2 \times 2\,1/4 \times 13$	2
4 FOOT PIN	$1/4$ DIAMETER $\times 2\,1/4$	4
5 RAIL PIN	$1/4$ DIAMETER $\times 2$	6

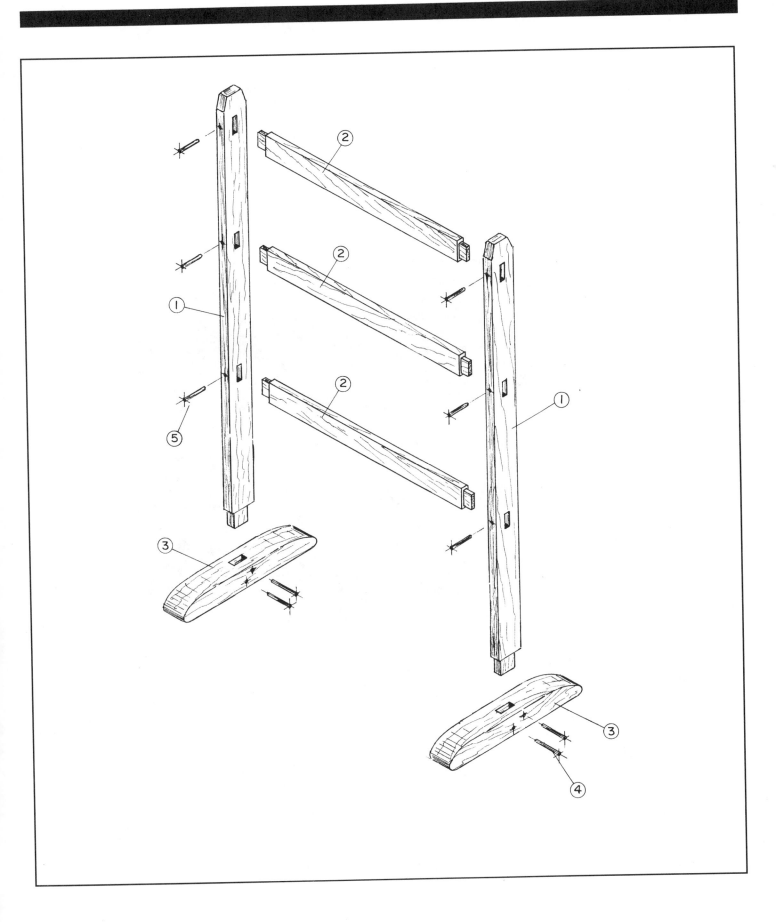

Elephant Pull Toy

Pictured is a gray elephant wearing a red blanket. Red wheels and a green base complete this early toy, which would amuse today's child just as much as it delighted boys and girls of an earlier time.

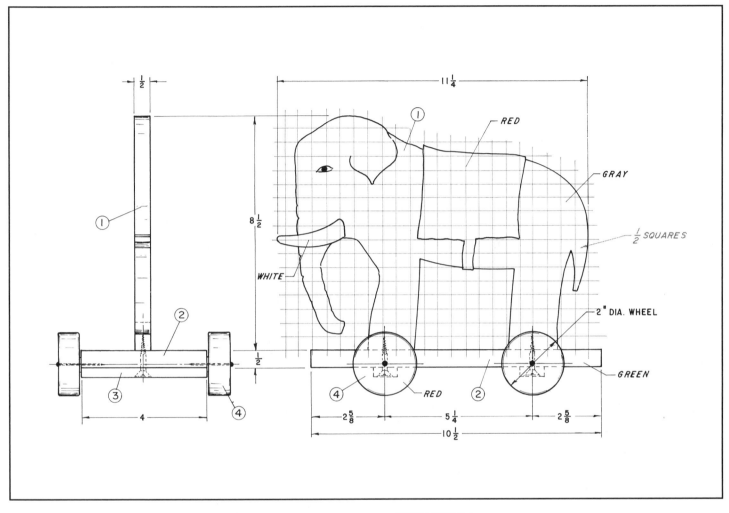

PART	INCHES	NEEDED
1 BODY	$\frac{1}{2} \times 8\frac{1}{2} \times 11\frac{1}{4}$	1
2 BASE	$\frac{1}{2} \times 4 \times 10\frac{1}{2}$	1
3 AXLE	$\frac{1}{4} \times 1 \times 4$	2
4 WHEEL	$\frac{3}{4} \times 2$ DIAMETER	4

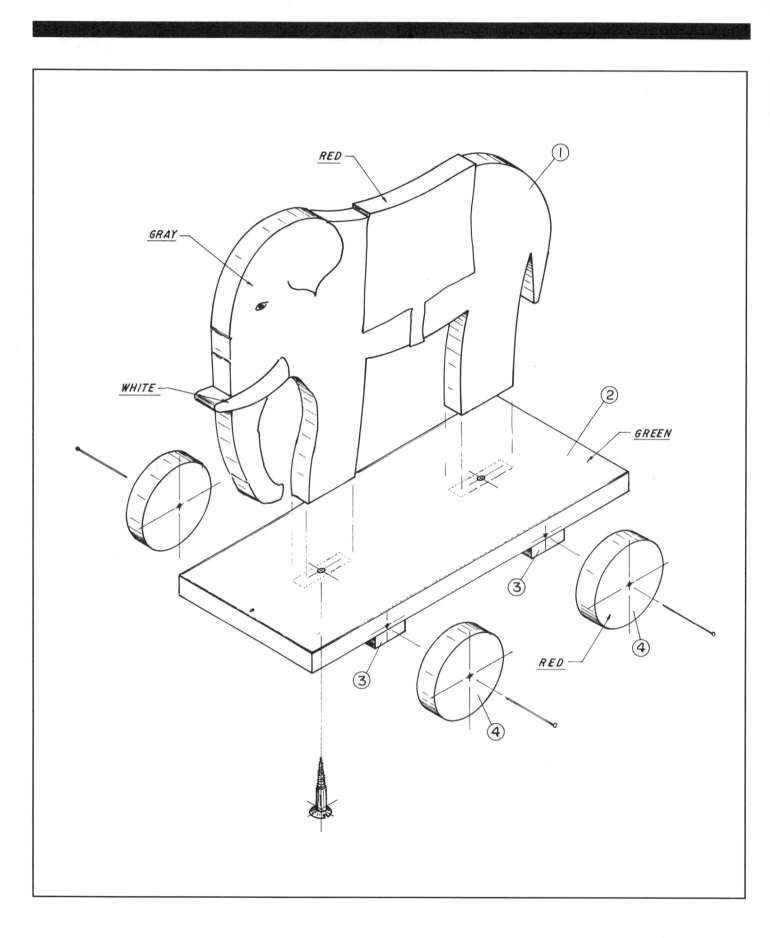

RED

GRAY

WHITE

①

②

GREEN

③

③

④

RED

④

42

Country Silver Tray

This silver tray is of a very early design, somewhat odd and rustic. The original was made of softwood, probably pine, and painted green; it was found in southern New England. The tray measures 9 inches deep by 14 inches wide by 5 inches high.

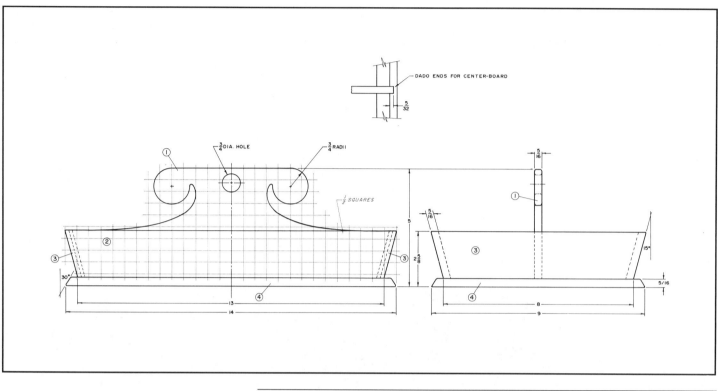

PART	INCHES	NEEDED
1 HANDLE	$5/16 \times 4^{11}/16 \times 13^{3}/4$	1
2 SIDE	$5/16 \times 2^{3}/8 \times 14$	2
3 END	$5/16 \times 2^{3}/8 \times 9$	2
4 BOTTOM	$5/16 \times 9 \times 14$	1

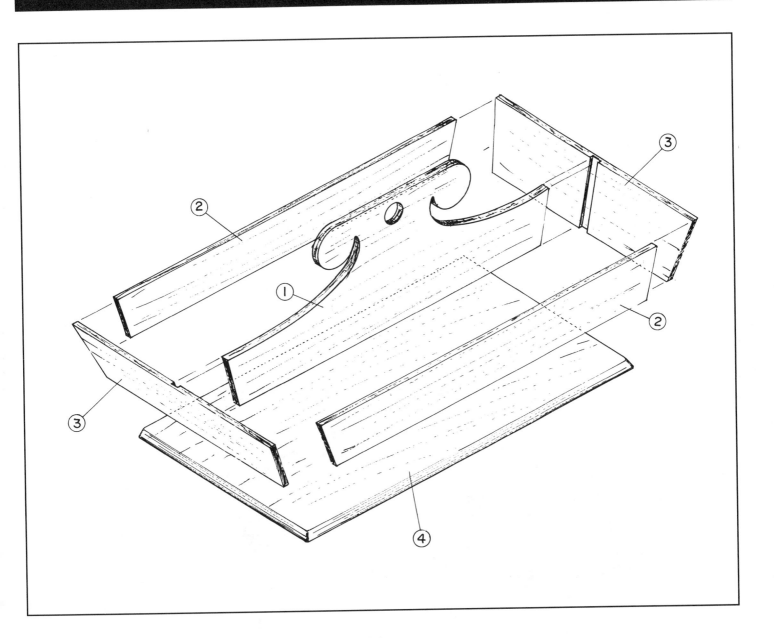

Silver Tray

Somewhat more formal than the preceding tray, this silver tray of stained pine was probably a late design. The original was found in Wakefield, Rhode Island. Silver trays can be used today for their original purpose. This one measures 10 inches deep by 14 inches wide by 7³/₄ inches high.

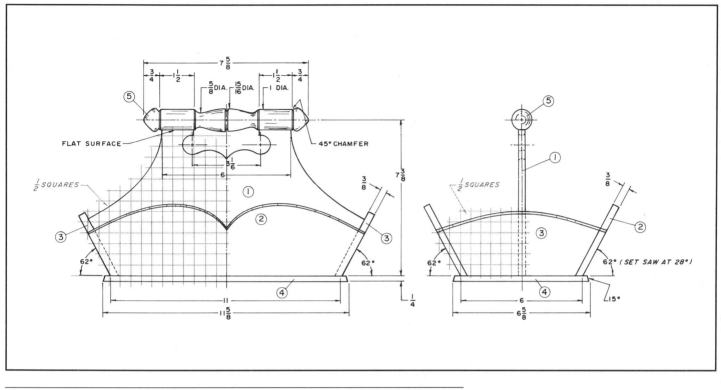

PART	INCHES	NEEDED
1 CENTER BOARD	$3/8 \times 7 \times 13$	1
2 SIDE	$3/8 \times 4 \times 13$	2
3 END	$3/8 \times 3^{1}/2 \times 8$	2
4 BOTTOM	$1/4 \times 6^{5}/8 \times 11^{5}/8$	1
5 HANDLE	1 DIAMETER $\times 7^{5}/8$	1

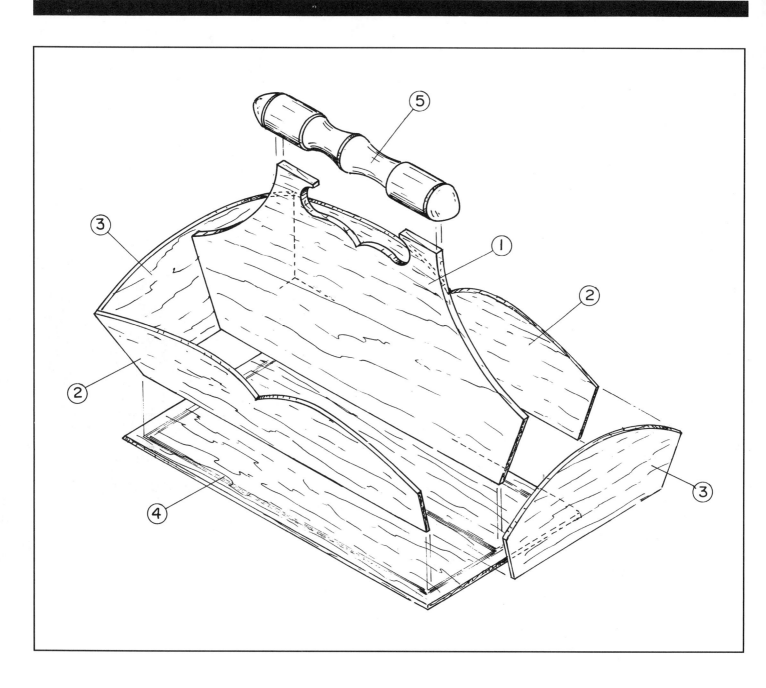

Dough Box

Dough boxes came in all sizes, usually much larger than this one. They were used to hold rising dough. The original probably had a lid, to keep out cold drafts, and was made of poplar, although any other hardwood except cherry could be used. Cherry reacts with the dough and makes it sour; cherry dough boxes are therefore extremely rare. This one was painted olive green with a painted grain effect. The original was found in Massachusetts. Measurements are 5 inches deep by 15 inches wide by 5 1/2 inches high.

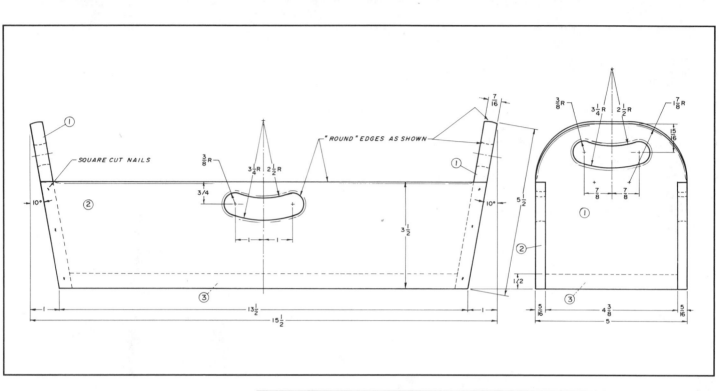

PART	INCHES	NEEDED
1 END	$^7/_{16} \times 5 \times 5^1/_2$	2
2 SIDE	$^5/_{16} \times 3^1/_2 \times 14^3/_4$	2
3 BOTTOM	$^1/_2 \times 4^3/_8 \times 12^7/_8$	1

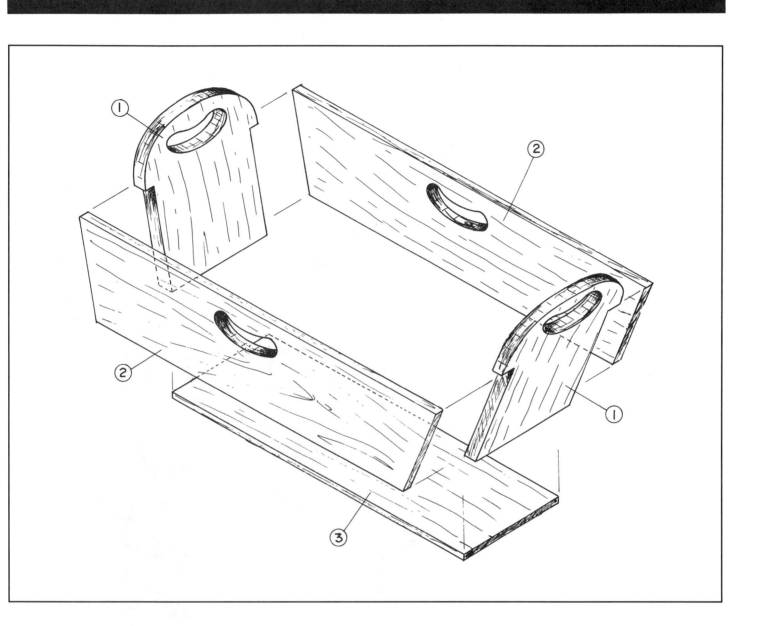

Country Watch Hutch

This New England design is of a very early watch hutch. It features dovetail construction and early snipe hinges. The original was made around 1740 of pine. The case is stained. This one measures 2³/₈ inches deep by 6¹/₄ inches wide by 7³/₈ inches high.

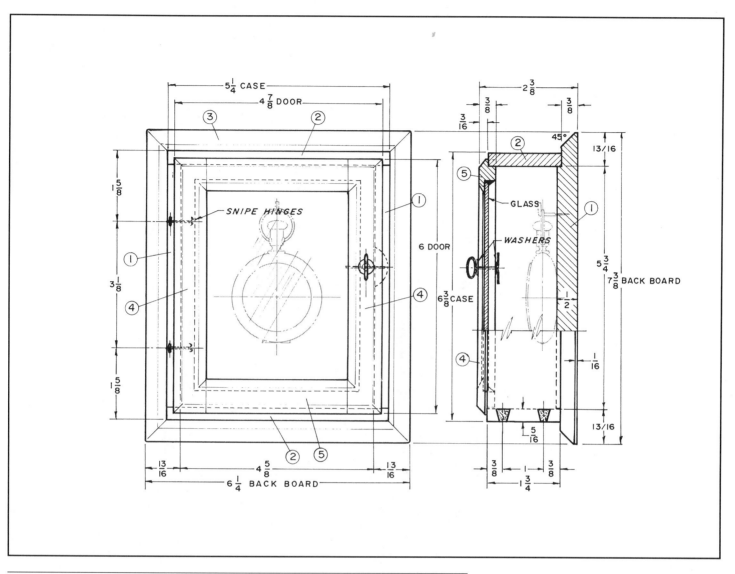

PART		INCHES	NEEDED
1	SIDE	$5/16 \times 1^3/4 \times 6^3/8$	2
2	TOP / BOTTOM	$5/16 \times 1^3/4 \times 5^1/4$	2
3	BACK BOARD	$1/2 \times 6^1/4 \times 7^3/8$	1
4	DOOR STILE	$3/8 \times 3/4 \times 6$	2
5	DOOR RAIL	$3/8 \times 3/4 \times 4^7/8$	2

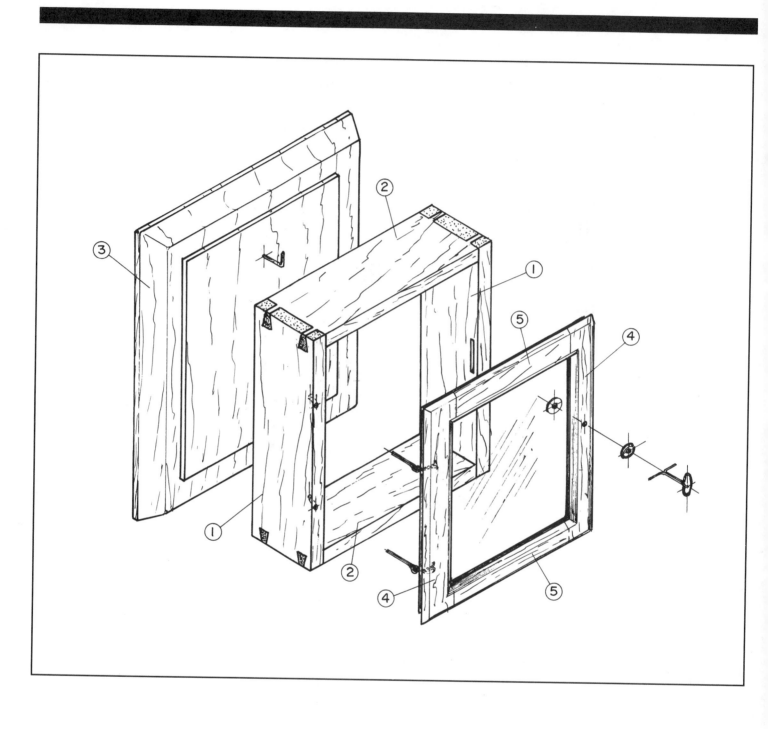

Formal Watch Hutch

A more formal design than the preceding example, this mahogany case has the tombstone cutout of an early (c. 1775) watch hutch. It has a mellow surface finish. Measurements are 1³/₈ inches deep by 5¹/₂ inches wide by 12¹/₂ inches high.

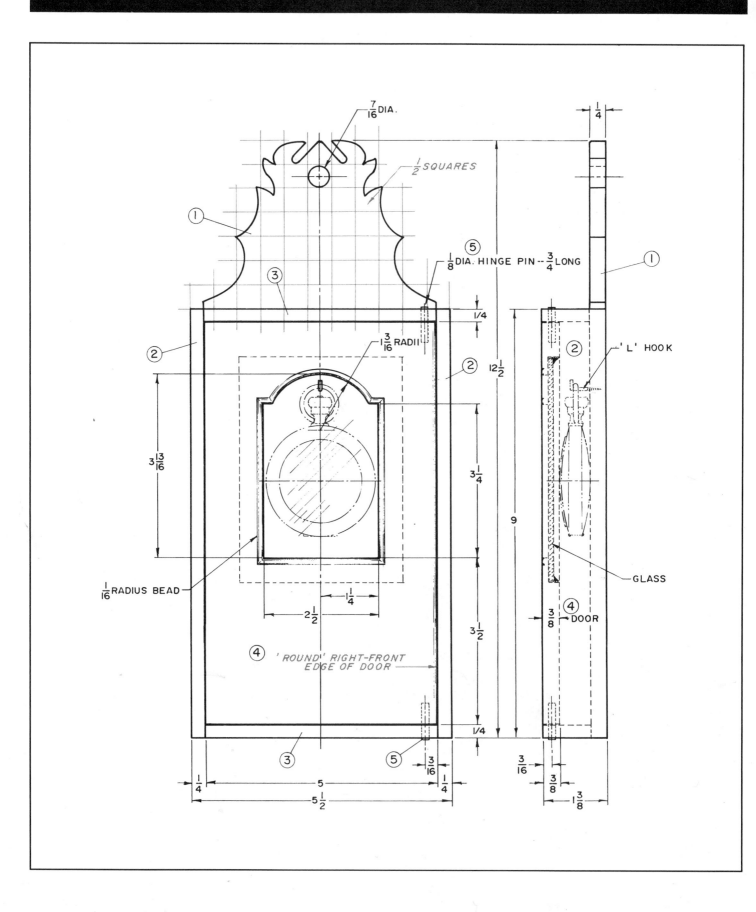

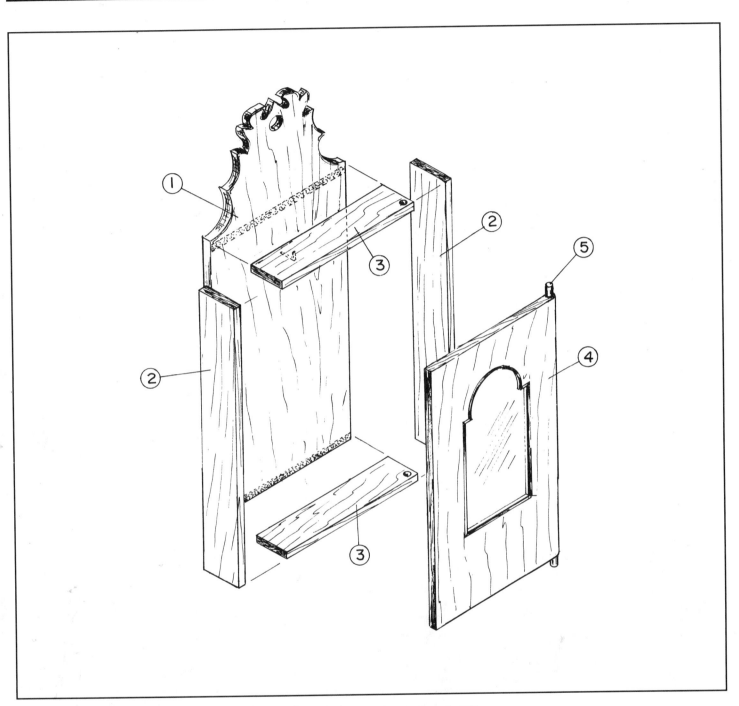

PART	INCHES	NEEDED
1 BACK BOARD	$1/4 \times 5 \times 12^{1}/_{2}$	1
2 SIDE	$1/4 \times 1^{3}/_{8} \times 9$	2
3 TOP / BOTTOM BOARD	$1/4 \times 1^{1}/_{8} \times 5$	2
4 DOOR	$3/8 \times 5 \times 8^{1}/_{2}$	1
5 PIN	$1/8 \times 3/4$	2

FOOTSTOOLS AND BENCHES

Footstools and benches came in all shapes and sizes—there are probably no two made exactly the same. Early settlers who had hammer and saw made their own stools, using whatever form they thought was best. Because of this, each early stool, no matter how crude, has a lot of character. Yet even these stools have certain features in common. They were usually simple three-legged affairs with plain tops. Most used butt joints nailed with square-cut nails and had cyma-curved sides and ends.

Later, simple ends, sides, and tops were used for the stools and benches we are familiar with today. Some stools were painted, but it is interesting to note that many stools from Vermont were painted all over except for the top board, which was stained.

Stools ranged from very formal to somewhat crude. They were made of all kinds of wood. Some even had rockers so that they could be used with rocking chairs; both chair and stool would rock together. Early footstools were referred to as "crickets."

Chairs were later developed from the basic designs of early stools.

Country Footstool

Every farmer had his own idea about what a footstool should look like. This one is a very early design, much larger than most. The original was of pine and was found in New England. The stool measures 5³/₄ inches deep by 13¹/₂ inches wide by 5³/₈ inches high.

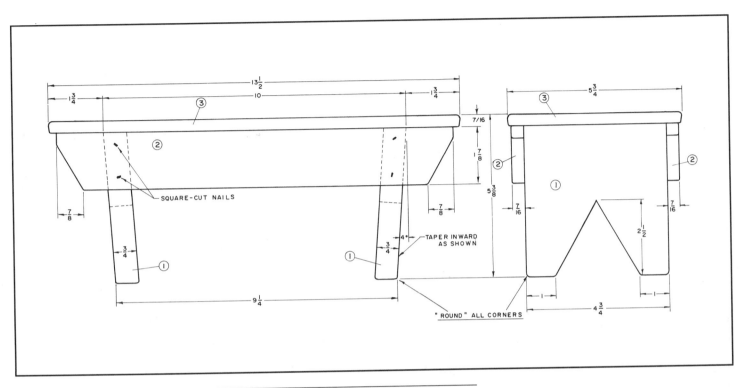

PART	INCHES	NEEDED
1 FOOT	3/4 × 4³/4 × 5	2
2 BRACE	7/16 × 1⁷/8 × 13	2
3 TOP	7/16 × 5³/4 × 13¹/2	1

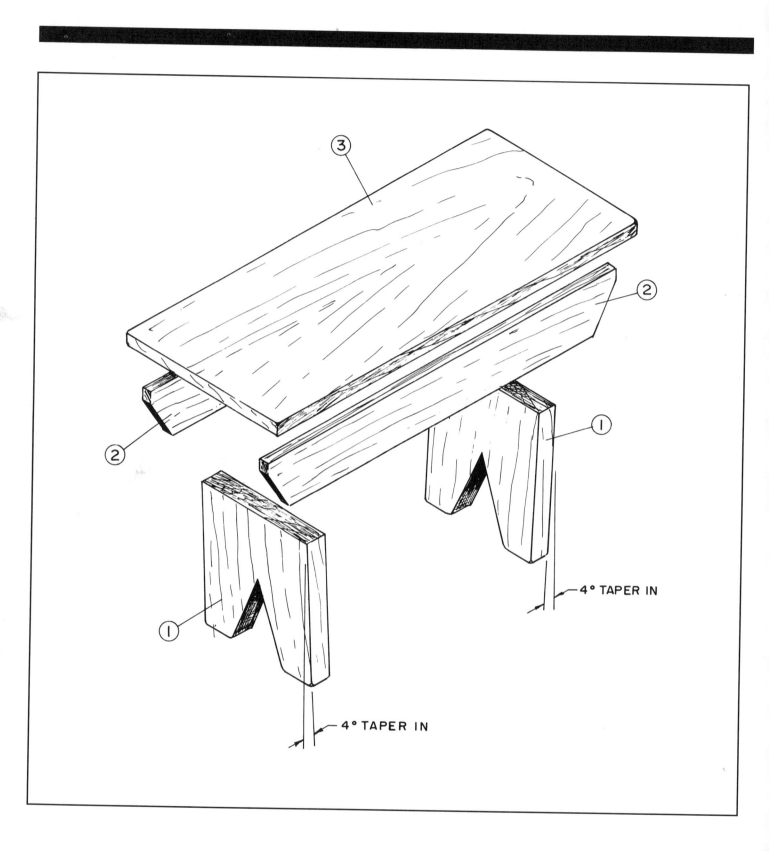

4° TAPER IN

4° TAPER IN

Vermont Footstool

This footstool (c.1820–1830) has arched cutouts, green painted legs, and a skirt. The top is stained. Dimensions are 5³/4 inches deep, 18³/4 inches wide, and 6¹/4 inches high.

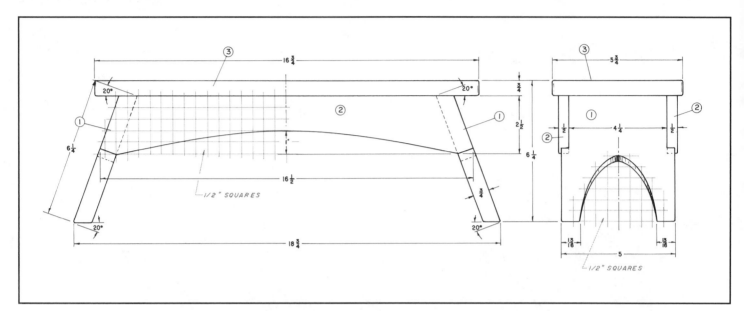

PART	INCHES	NEEDED
1 LEG	³⁄₄ × 5 × 6¹⁄₄	2
2 BRACE	¹⁄₂ × 2¹⁄₂ × 16¹⁄₂	2
3 TOP	³⁄₄ × 5³⁄₄ × 16³⁄₄	1

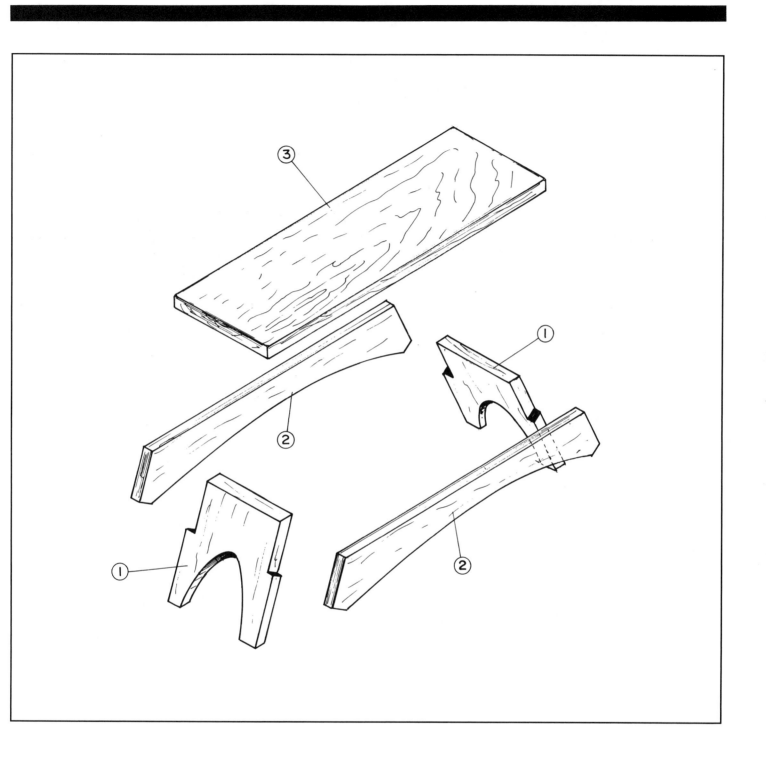

Kneeling Stool

This unusual stool, made to be kneeled upon, has a stained top, red painted legs, and a red apron. The original is from Vermont. It measures 7$\frac{1}{2}$ inches deep by 44 inches wide by 7 inches high.

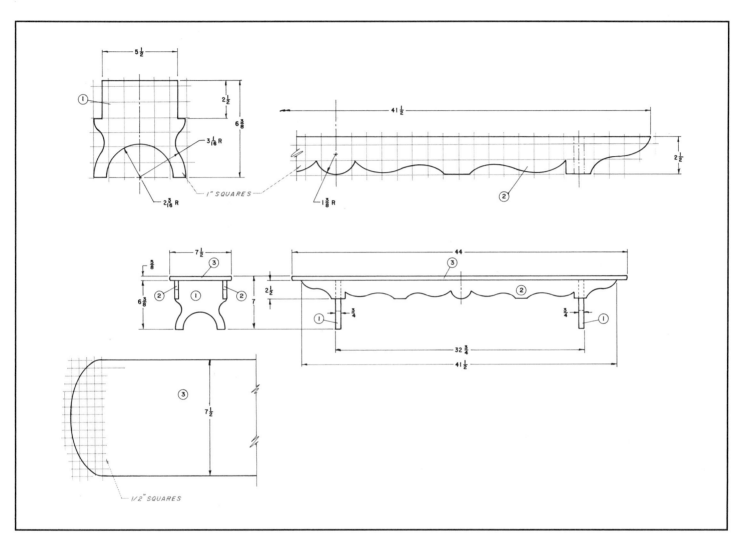

PART	INCHES	NEEDED
1 LEG	$3/4 \times 6^1/8 \times 6^3/8$	2
2 BRACE	$1/2 \times 2^1/2 \times 41^1/2$	2
3 TOP BOARD	$5/8 \times 7^1/2 \times 44$	1

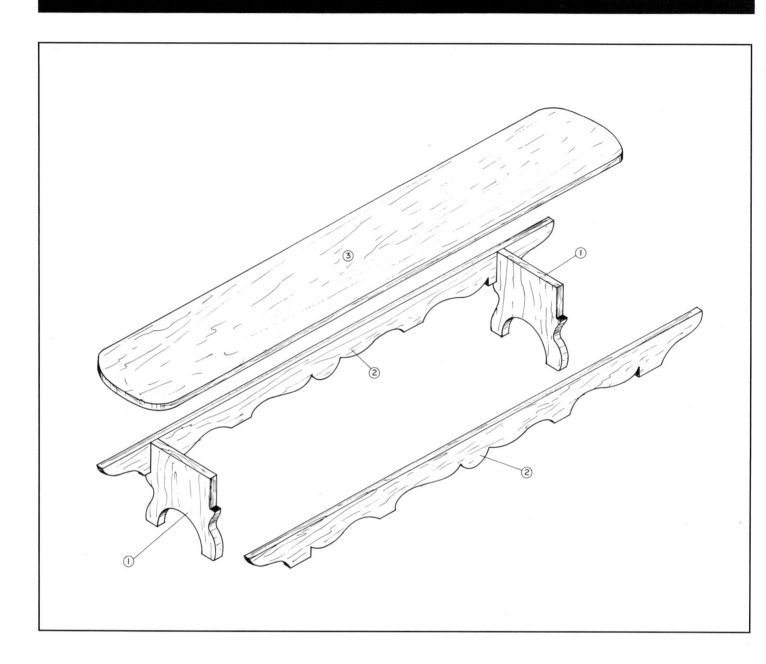

Large Stool

This is a good example of a five-board stool. Similar stools with the same general design were made as wide as 3 feet. This one measures 8 inches deep by 19½ inches wide by 9 inches high.

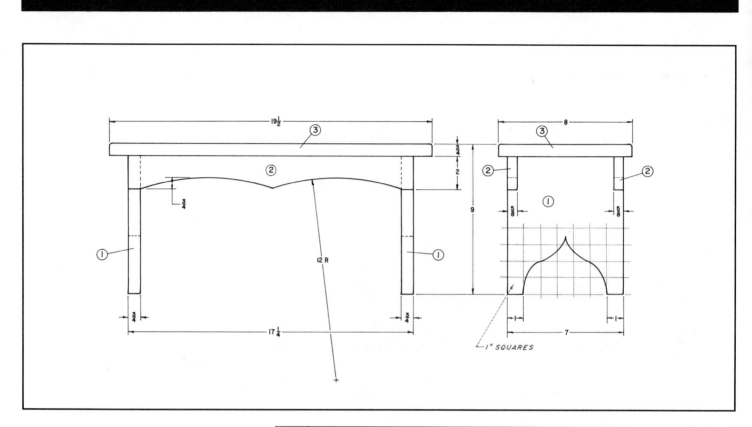

	PART	INCHES	NEEDED
1	FOOT	$^3/_4 \times 7 \times 8^1/_4$	2
2	TRIM	$^5/_8 \times 2 \times 17^1/_4$	2
3	TOP BOARD	$^3/_4 \times 8 \times 19^1/_2$	1

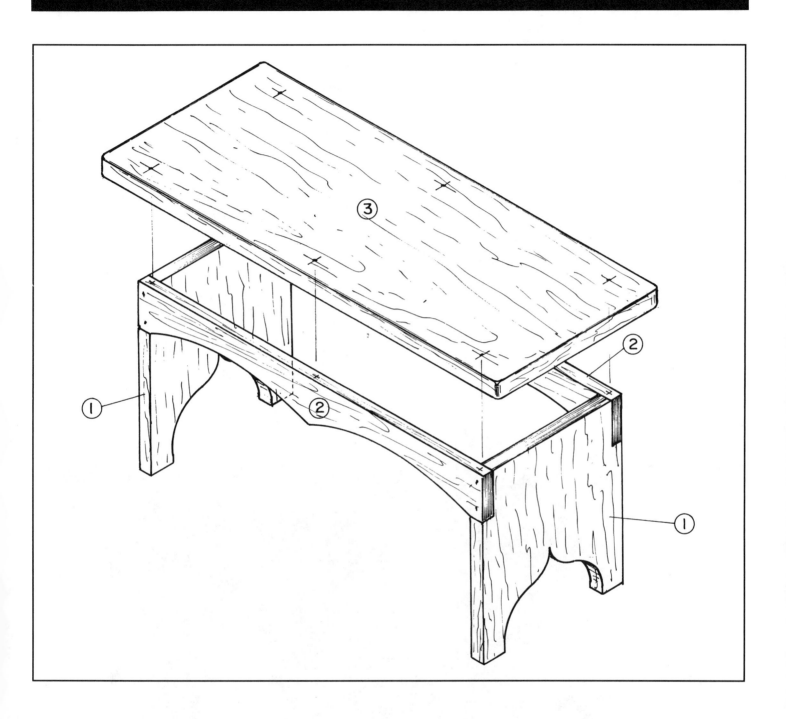

DESK BOXES

Desk boxes were nothing more than scaled-down, six-board blanket chests. They were used to store everything from jewelry to toys—even that very expensive commodity, tea. Some had partitions designed for particular items. Many early desk boxes had built-in locks, not to protect valuable jewelry but to safeguard the family Bible. In those days the Bible contained a record of the family—births, deaths, marriages—so it was especially important. Desk boxes were often painted, and some had designs painted on them. Many date to 1675 or earlier.

Miniature Blanket Chest

This desk box, a miniature mahogany blanket chest, has dovetail construction. Probably designed around 1825, it is of unknown origin. Measurements are 4³/8 inches deep by 8 inches wide by 5¹/4 inches high.

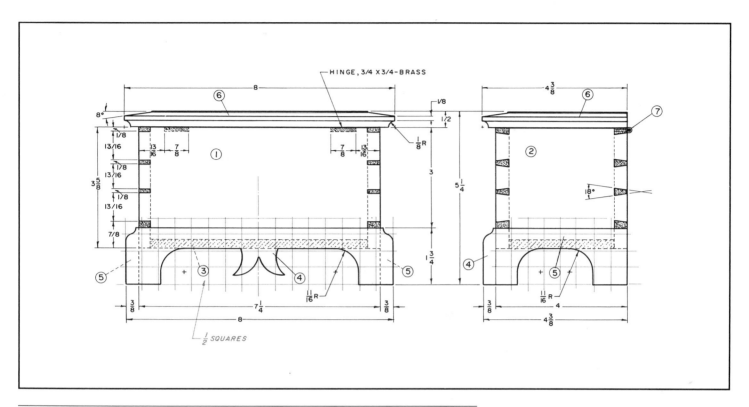

PART	INCHES	NEEDED
1 FRONT	$3/8 \times 3^5/8 \times 7^1/4$	2
2 END	$3/8 \times 3^5/8 \times 4$	2
3 BOTTOM	$1/4 \times 3^1/4 \times 6^1/2$	1
4 FRONT TRIM	$3/8 \times 1^3/4 \times 8$	1
5 SIDE TRIM	$3/8 \times 1^3/4 \times 4$	2
6 LID	$1/2 \times 4^3/8 \times 8$	1
7 BRASS HINGE	$3/4 \times 7/8$	2

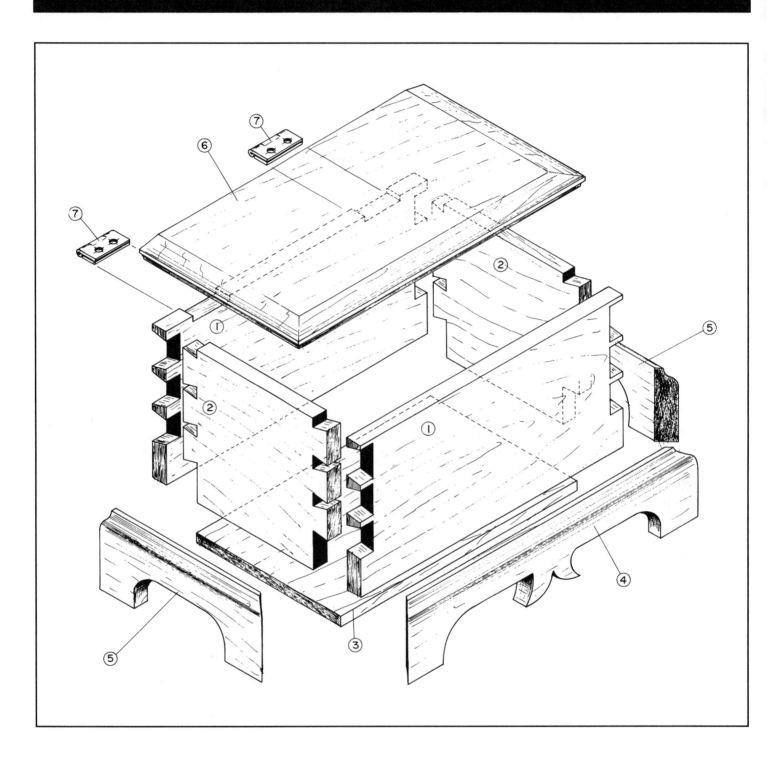

Miniature Chest

This small chest, intended to be a desk box, has a lock and a very unusual base. The original was painted green and probably made of pine. Its origin is unknown. The chest measures 6^1/$_2$ inches deep by 13^1/$_4$ inches wide by 8^3/$_4$ inches high.

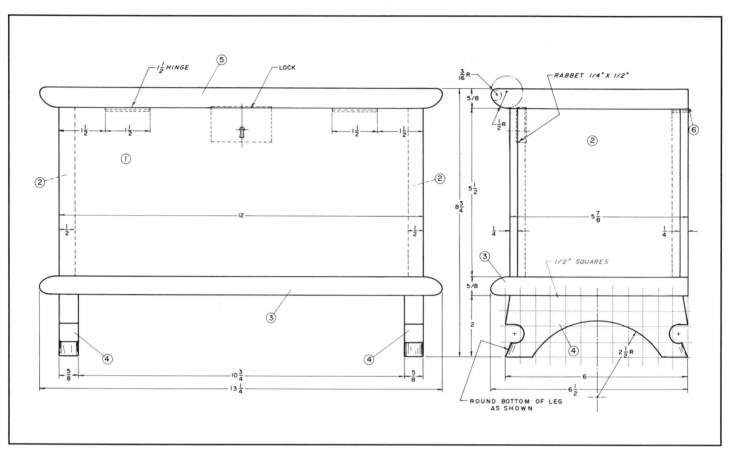

PART	INCHES	NEEDED
1 FRONT / BACK	$1/2 \times 5^{1}/_2 \times 12$	2
2 SIDE	$1/2 \times 5^{1}/_2 \times 5^{3}/_8$	2
3 BOTTOM	$5/8 \times 6^{1}/_2 \times 13^{1}/_4$	1
4 LEG	$5/8 \times 2 \times 6^{1}/_2$	2
5 LID	$5/8 \times 6^{1}/_2 \times 13^{1}/_4$	1
6 BRASS HINGE	$1^{1}/_4 \times 1^{1}/_2$	2

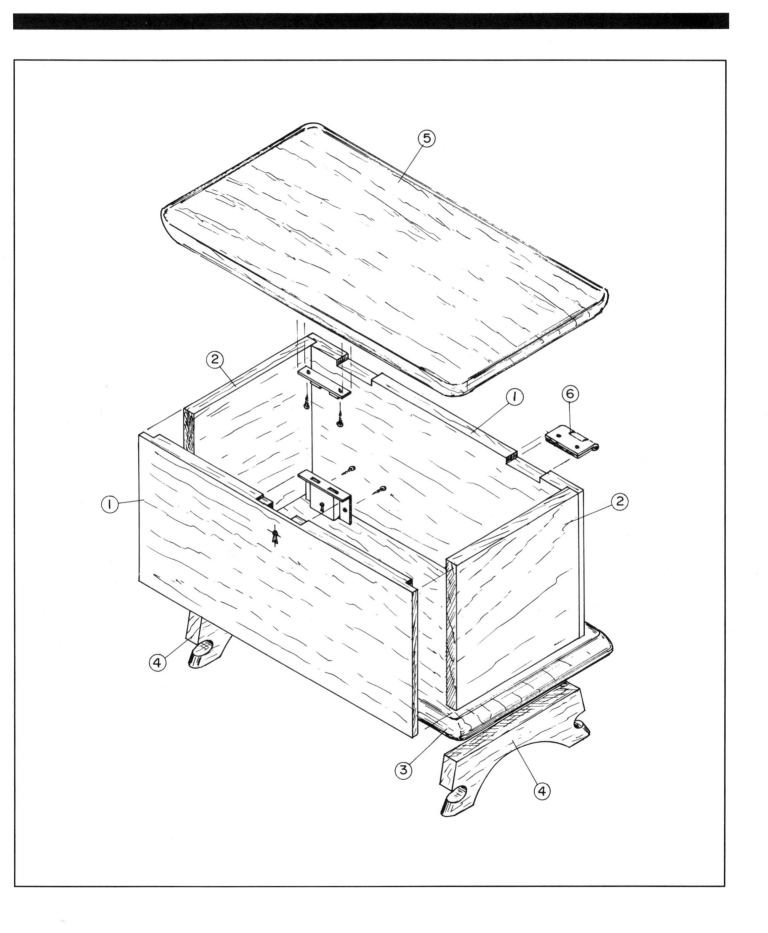

Document Box

Maple was used for this dovetailed box. The reproduction looks old because the maple was rough and wormy. The original came from southern New Hampshire. The box measures 6½ inches deep by 12⅛ inches wide by 6¾ inches high.

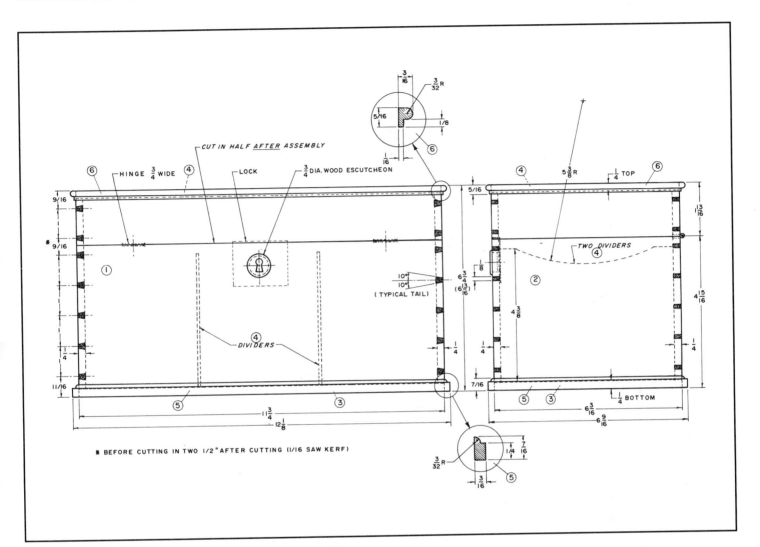

PART		INCHES	NEEDED
1	FRONT / BACK	1/4 × 6 5/16 × 11 3/4	2
2	SIDE	1/4 × 6 5/16 × 6 3/16	2
3	BOTTOM	1/4 × 6 3/16 × 11 3/4	1
4	OPTIONAL DIVIDER	3/32 × 4 3/8 × 5 11/16	2
5	SKIRT	3/16 × 7/16 × 40	1
6	TRIM	3/16 × 5/16 × 40	1
7	BRASS HINGE	1/2 × 3/4	2
8	LOCK	TO SUIT	1
9	WOODEN ESCUTCHEON	3/4 DIAMETER	2

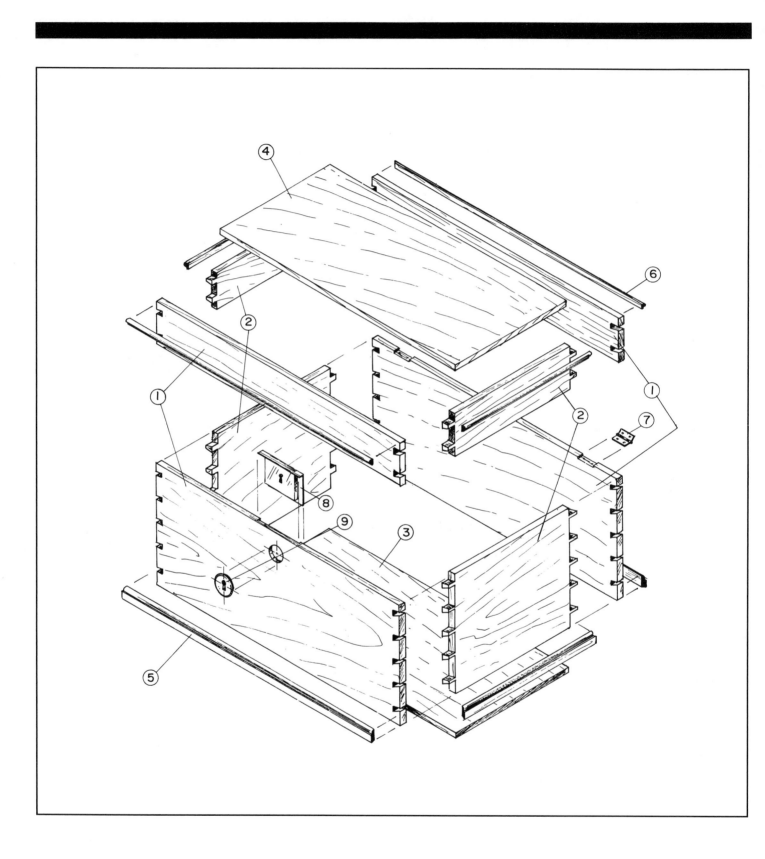

Small Jewelry Box

For the lid, the original used wooden dowel hinges, a feature seldom found on such a small box. Made of hardwood, probably maple or poplar, the box was found in northern New England and measures 4¹⁄8 inches deep by 6¹⁄4 inches wide by 4¹⁄8 inches high.

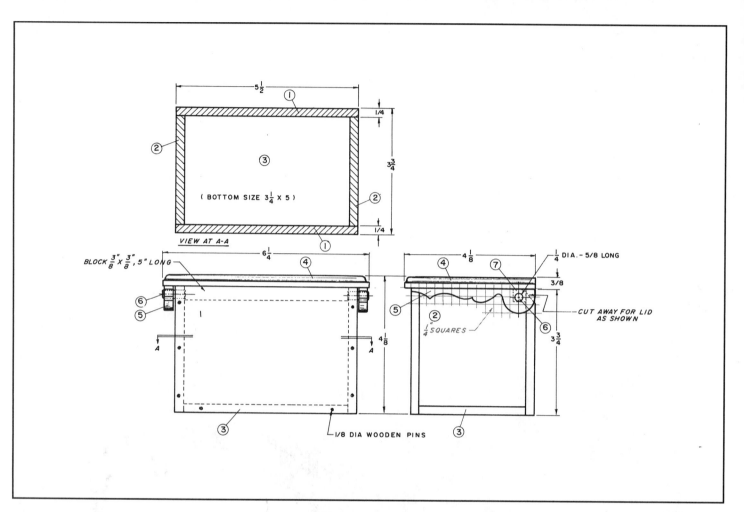

PART		INCHES	NEEDED
1	FRONT / BACK	$1/4 \times 3^{3}/4 \times 5^{1}/2$	2
2	SIDE	$1/4 \times 3^{1}/2 \times 5^{1}/2$	2
3	BOTTOM	$1/4 \times 3^{1}/4 \times 5^{1}/2$	1
4	LID	$3/8 \times 4^{1}/8 \times 6^{1}/4$	1
5	HINGE	$1/4 \times 3/4 \times 3^{3}/4$	2
6	PIN	$1/4$ DIAMETER $\times 5/8$	2
7	DUST STOP	$3/8$ SQUARE $\times 5$	1

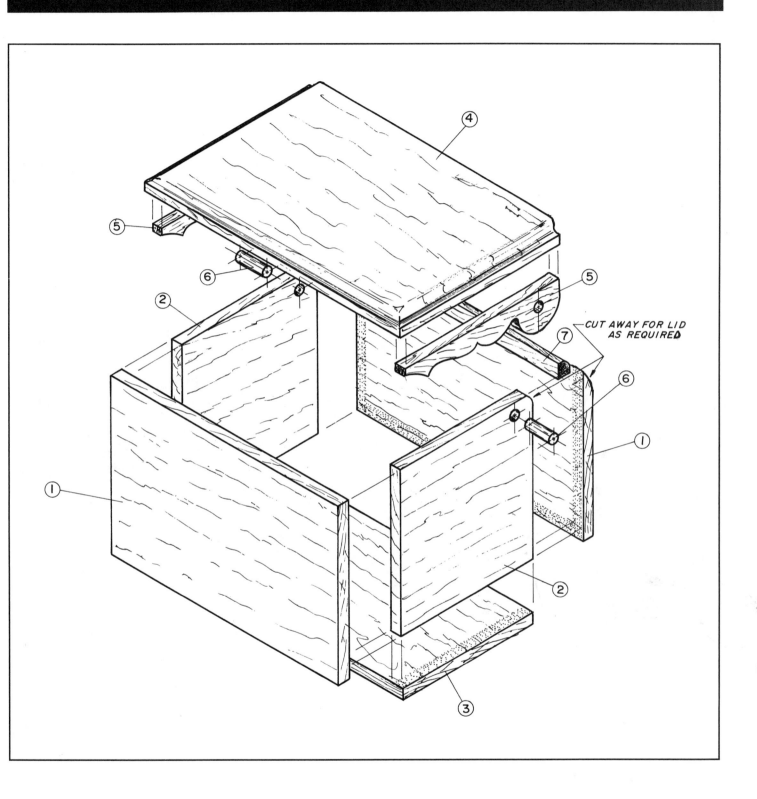

CUT AWAY FOR LID
AS REQUIRED

Fire Engine Equipment Box

This interesting box is designed after one from the Governor Bradford fire station in northern New England. The original was used to store fire-fighting equipment and was painted with a red background, green shadows, and gold decorated letters. The directions here are for making the box at half its original size (with the original dimensions shown in parentheses). Scaled down, the box measures $4\frac{1}{2}$ inches deep by $13\frac{1}{2}$ inches wide by $3\frac{9}{16}$ inches high.

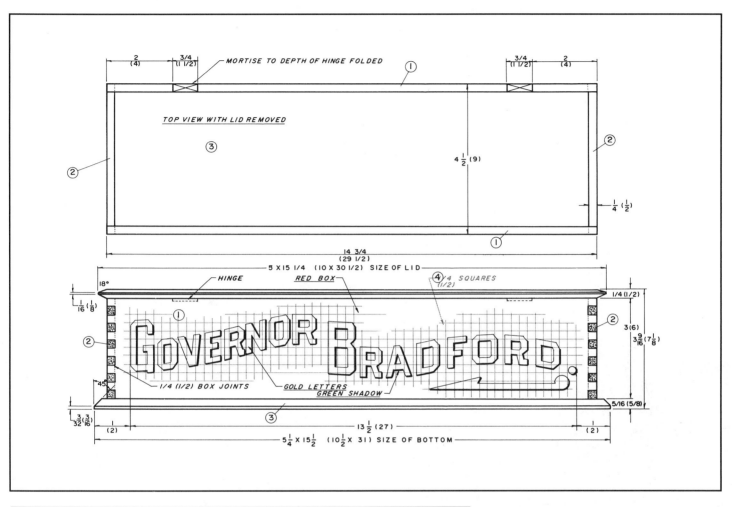

PART		INCHES	NEEDED
1	FRONT / BACK	$1/4 \times 3 \times 14^{3/4}$	2
2	SIDE	$1/4 \times 3 \times 4$	2
3	BOTTOM	$5/16 \times 5^{1/4} \times 15^{1/2}$	1
4	LID	$1/4 \times 5 \times 15^{1/4}$	1
5	BRASS HINGE	$1/2 \times 3/4$	2

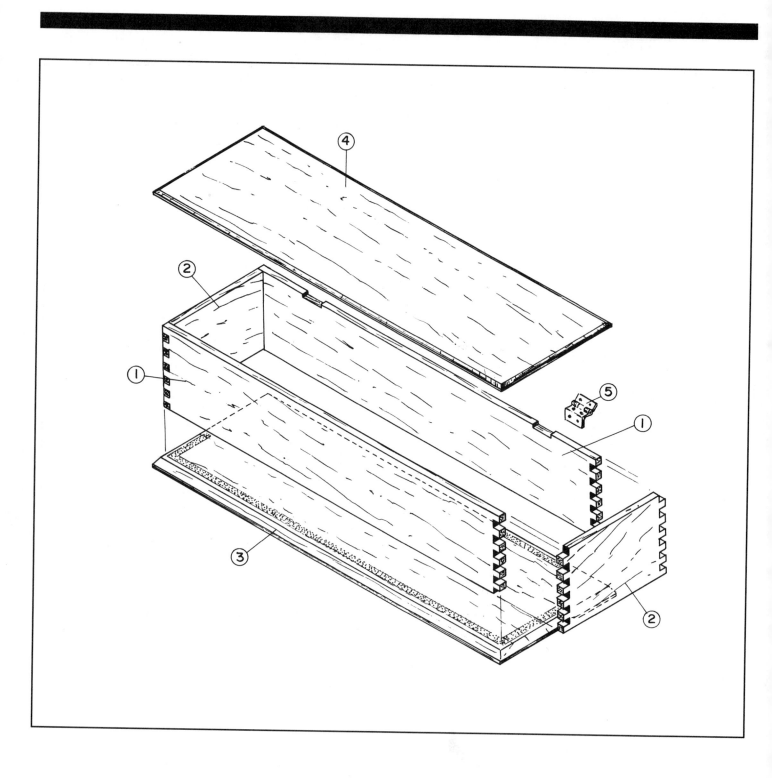

Trinket Box

Small boxes like this one were used to store all kinds of things, as the name suggests. The original box (*c.* 1825) was painted blue and had unusual red and white compass designs scratched into the sides and lid. Found in Lancaster County, Pennsylvania, it was held together with wooden pegs, tin hinges, and a tin hasp. The hardware can be made by cutting the pieces from a large tin can (use a pair of heavy scissors) and then bending them to shape. The wire parts are made from a coat hanger. To give the hardware an old look, heat it with a torch until it is blue and let it cool. This is called *blueing*. The dark color will make the metal look very old. Measurements are 4 inches deep by 5¹⁄₂ inches wide by 5 inches high.

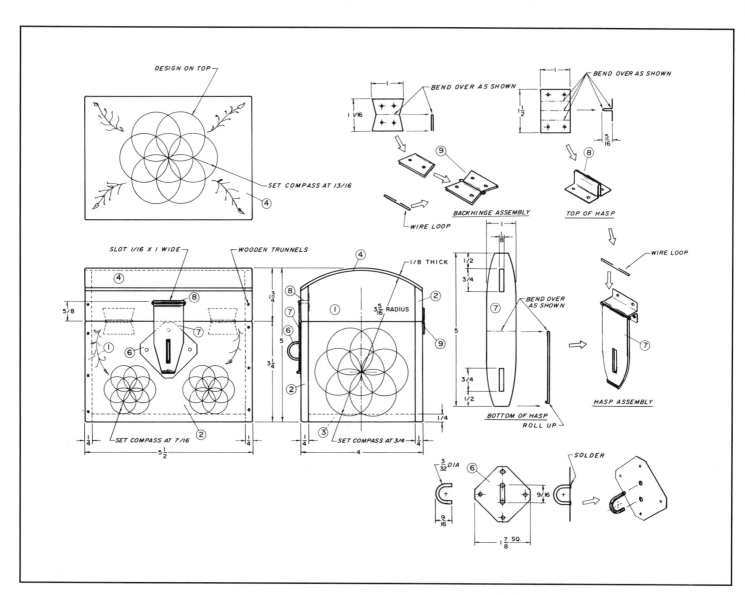

PART		INCHES	NEEDED
1	END	$1/4 \times 3^1/2 \times 4^7/8$	2
2	FRONT	$1/4 \times 4^1/2 \times 5^1/2$	2
3	BOTTOM	$1/4 \times 3^1/2 \times 5$	1
4	TOP	$1/8 \times 4^3/4 \times 5^1/2$	1
5	PIN	$3/32$ DIAMETER $\times 1/2$	16
6	"U"	$1/32 \times 1^7/8$ SQUARE	2
7	LATCH	$1/32 \times 1 \times 5$	1
8	LATCH HINGE	$1/32 \times 1 \times 1^1/2$	1
9	HINGE	$1/32 \times 1 \times 1^1/16$	2

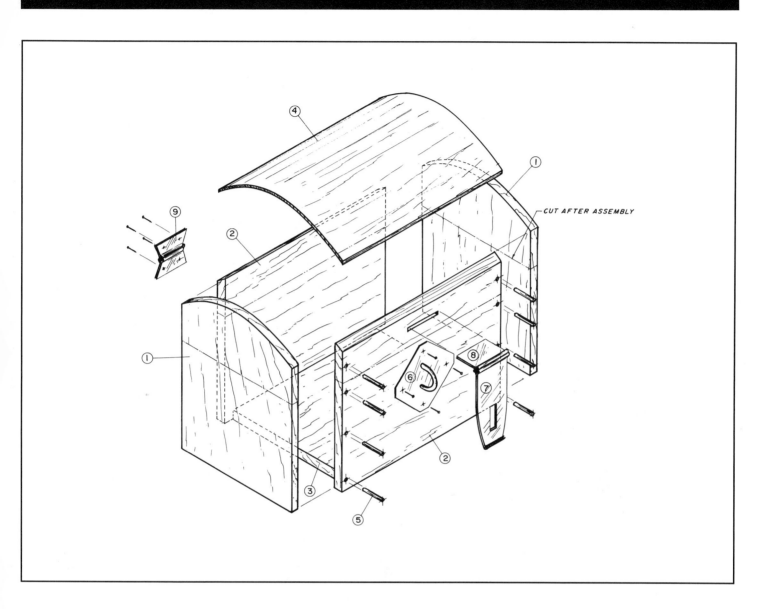

CUT AFTER ASSEMBLY

Slant-Lid Desk Box

The original of this lap desk came from Vermont. Made around 1815, it was painted red with black streaks to simulate wood grain and had three turnip feet. It measures 9½ inches deep by 8½ inches wide by 9 inches high.

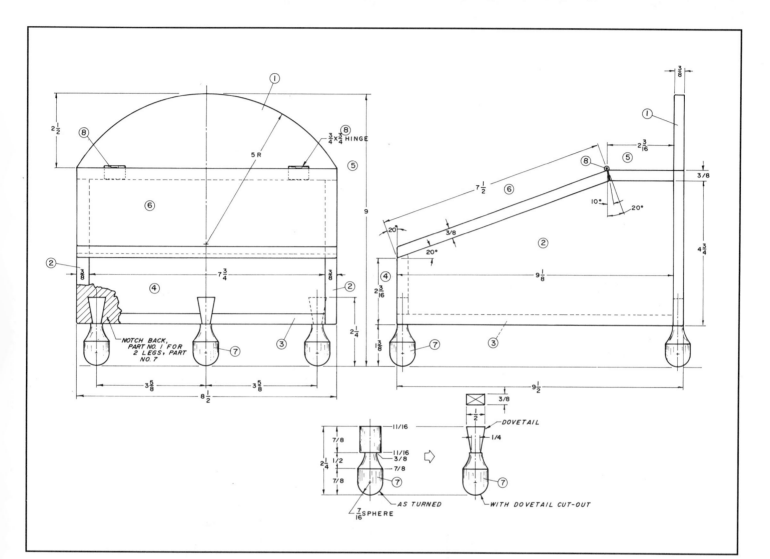

PART		INCHES	NEEDED
1	BACK	$3/8 \times 7^5/8 \times 8^1/2$	1
2	SIDE	$3/8 \times 4^3/4 \times 9^1/8$	2
3	BOTTOM	$3/8 \times 9^1/8 \times 7^3/4$	1
4	FRONT	$3/8 \times 2 \times 7^3/4$	1
5	TOP	$3/8 \times 2^3/16 \times 8^1/2$	1
6	LID	$3/8 \times 7^1/2 \times 8^1/2$	1
7	FOOT	$7/8$ DIAMETER $\times 2^1/4$	3
8	BRASS HINGE	$3/4 \times 3/4$	2

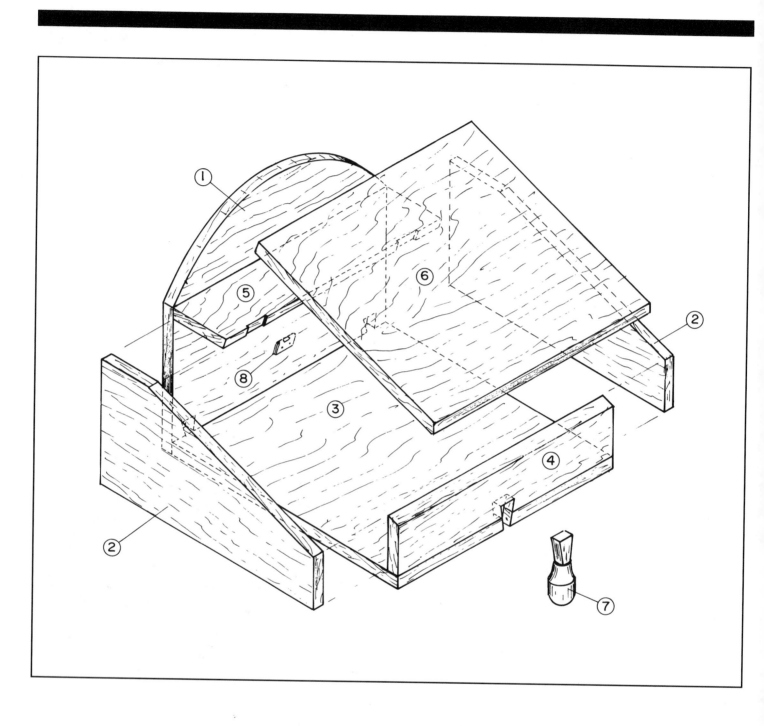

Desk Candle Box

A candle box of formal design, the original was made of walnut and found at Valley Forge, Pennsylvania. Note that the lines are similar to those of the salt box (page 160), even though the salt box was found in New Hampshire. Measurements are 4³/4 inches deep by 12 inches wide by 8¹/2 inches high.

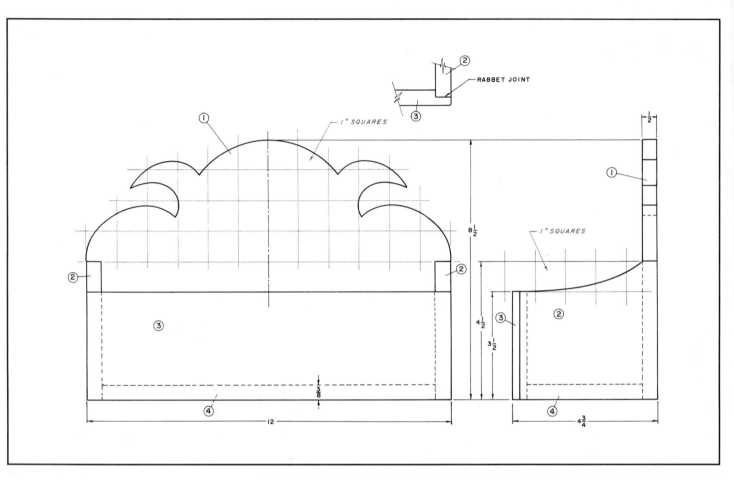

PART	INCHES	NEEDED
1 BACK BOARD	1/2 × 8 1/2 × 12	1
2 SIDE	1/2 × 4 1/2 × 4 1/2	2
3 FRONT	1/2 × 3 1/2 × 12	1
4 BOTTOM	1/2 × 3 3/4 × 11	1

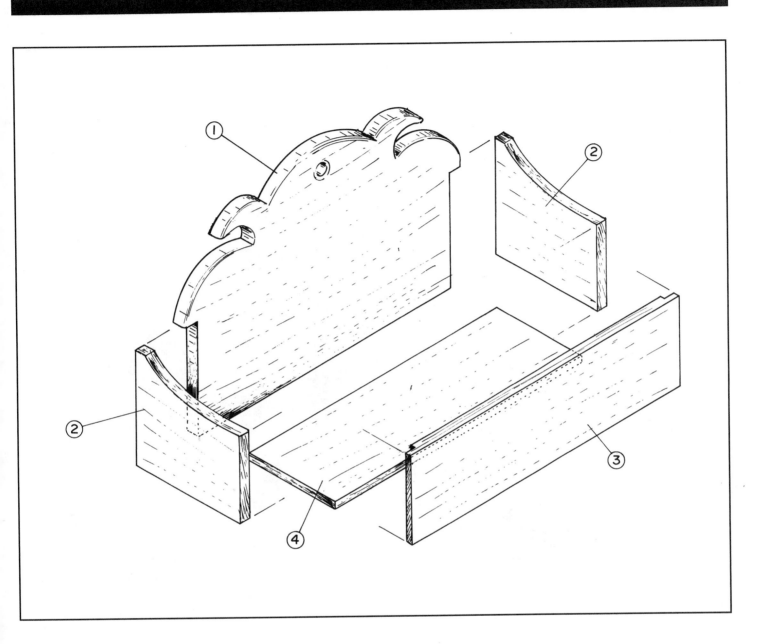

Shelf Box

This project is an example of a large box with two feet. It is larger than most boxes of the period, but the design is interesting. It measures 8 inches deep by 15 inches wide by 11½ inches high.

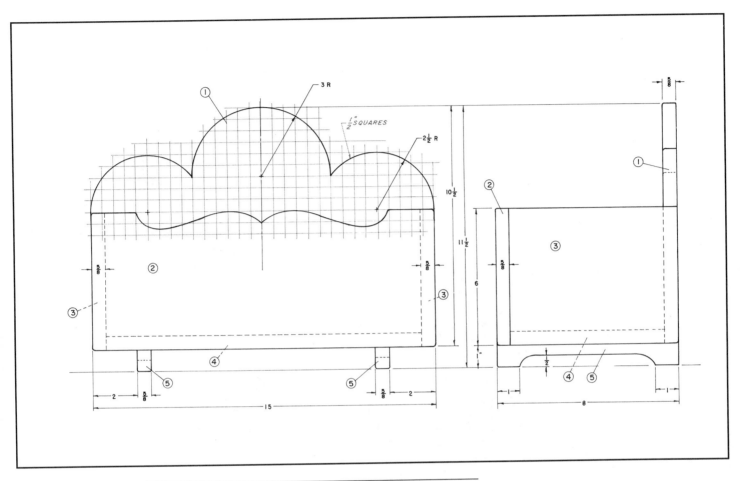

PART	INCHES	NEEDED
1 BACK BOARD	⅝ × 10½ × 15	1
2 FRONT	⅝ × 6 × 15	1
3 SIDE	⅝ × 6 × 7½	2
4 BOTTOM	⅝ × 7 × 14	1
5 FOOT	⅝ × 1 × 8	2

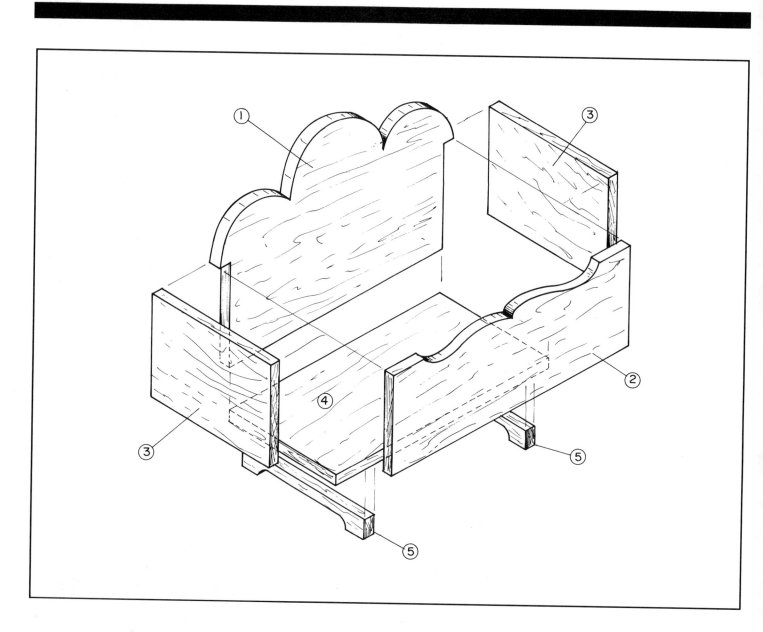

CANDLE BOXES

In years past, when candles were a necessity, small boxes in which to store them came in many shapes and forms. Some had sliding lids, some had hinged lids, and others had no lids at all. Many of the boxes used only leather straps as hinges. Other candle boxes hung on the wall with pegs or nails. It was said that candle boxes were often used to store jewelry and other valuables. They probably offered great hiding places—who would look for jewelry in a lowly candle box? Today the originals of these candle boxes command hefty prices. All kinds of woods were used in making them. Most sliding-lid boxes were made of hardwood, whereas those to be hung on the wall were made of pine. Candle boxes were usually painted, and the originals are now well worn. You may therefore want to try antiquing the paint finish on your reproductions.

Early Candle Box

Many early candle boxes had flat tops. This one has an interesting chamfered sliding top with three finger pulls carved into the lid. The original box (c. 1800) was nailed with rosehead nails and painted green; it was found in New England. Like most candle boxes meant to sit on a desk or table, it is made of hardwood. Measurements are 5^1/$_2$ inches deep by 12 inches wide by 4^1/$_2$ inches high.

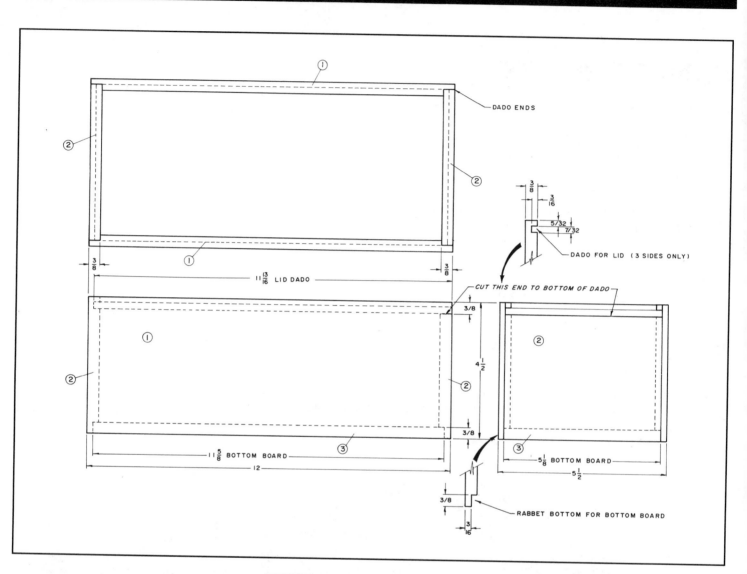

DADO ENDS

DADO FOR LID (3 SIDES ONLY)

$11\frac{13}{16}$ LID DADO

CUT THIS END TO BOTTOM OF DADO

$11\frac{5}{8}$ BOTTOM BOARD

12

$5\frac{1}{8}$ BOTTOM BOARD

$5\frac{1}{2}$

RABBET BOTTOM FOR BOTTOM BOARD

PART		INCHES	NEEDED
1	SIDE	$\frac{3}{8} \times 4\frac{1}{2} \times 12$	2
2	END	$\frac{3}{8} \times 4\frac{1}{2} \times 5\frac{1}{8}$	2
3	BOTTOM	$\frac{3}{8} \times 5\frac{1}{8} \times 11\frac{5}{8}$	1
4	LID	$\frac{3}{8} \times 5\frac{1}{16} \times 11\frac{5}{8}$	1

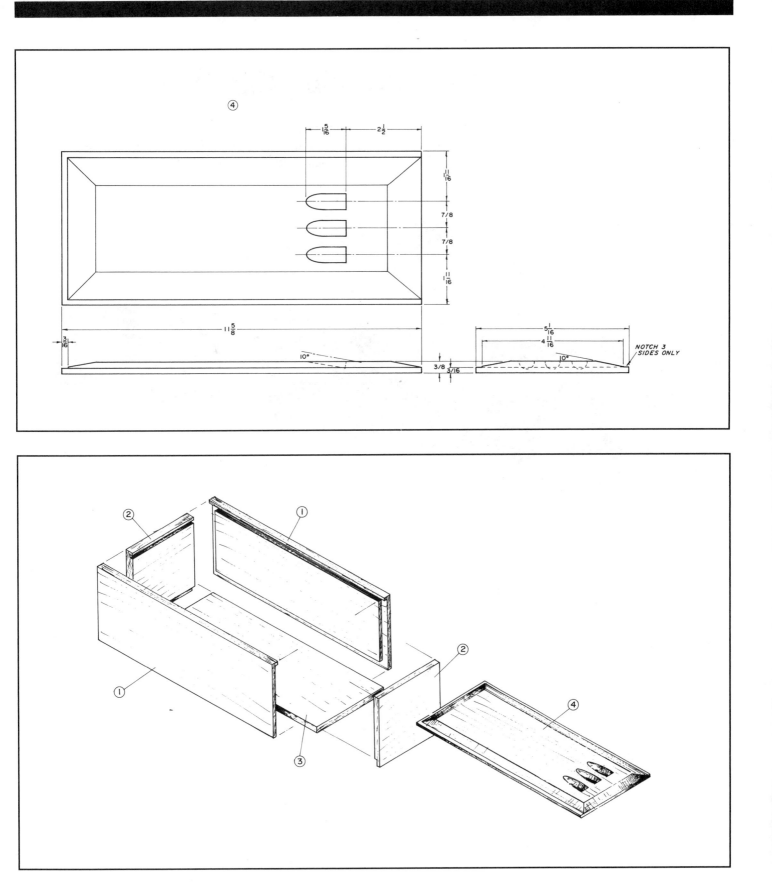

Wall-Hanging Candle Box

The original had leather strap hinges, not the metal butt hinges of the copy. Made of pine, it was found in New Hampshire. Dimensions are 5⅝ inches deep by 15½ inches wide by 6 inches high.

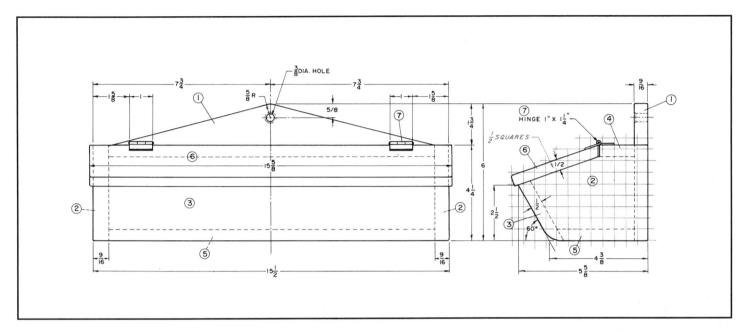

PART		INCHES	NEEDED
1	BACK	$^9/_{16} \times 6 \times 15^1/_2$	1
2	SIDE	$^1/_2 \times 4^1/_4 \times 5^5/_8$	2
3	FRONT	$^1/_2 \times 2^3/_8 \times 15^1/_2$	1
4	LIP SUPPORT	$^1/_2 \times 1^1/_8 \times 15^1/_2$	1
5	BOTTOM	$^1/_2 \times 2^1/_2 \times 14^3/_8$	1
6	LID	$^1/_2 \times 3^1/_{16} \times 15^5/_8$	1
7	STEEL HINGE	$1 \times 1^1/_4$	2

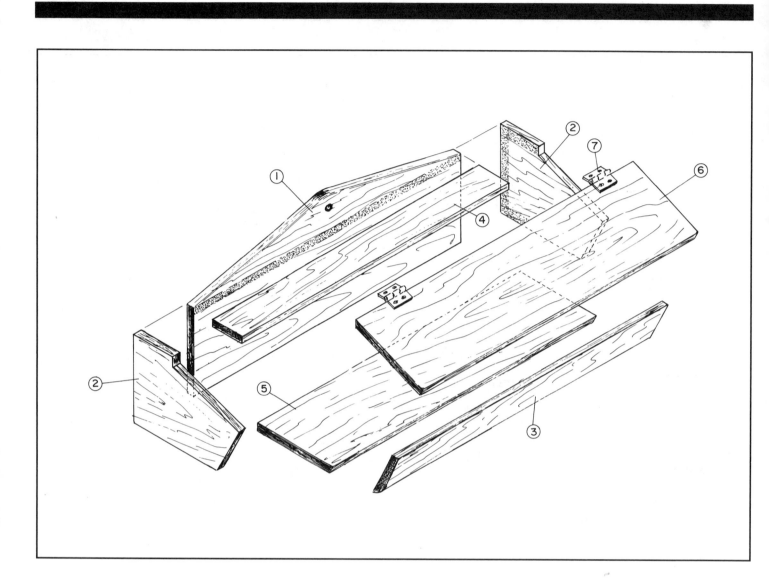

Country Candle Box

This box, though in the style of a candle box, is larger than most. The original may therefore have been used for something other than candles. It had a rough, worn, painted finish, which I have tried to duplicate in this reproduction. It measures 7 inches deep by 10¹/₄ inches wide by 14¹/₂ inches high.

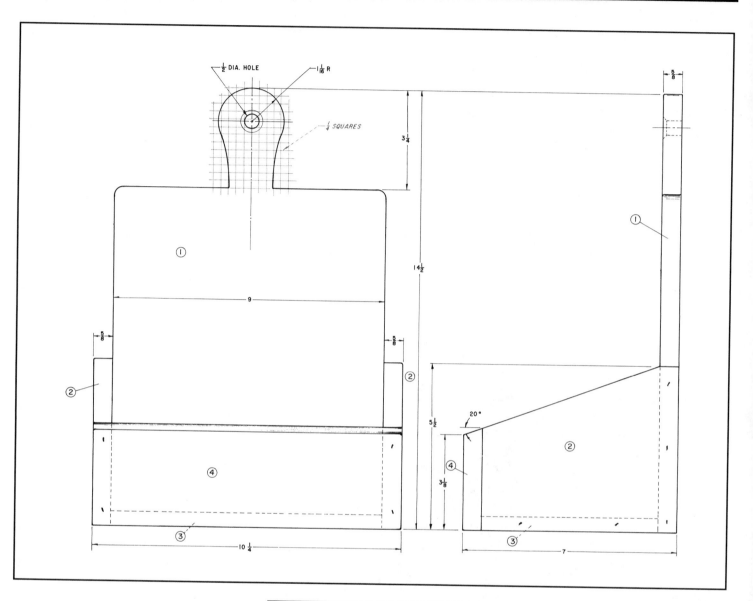

PART		INCHES	NEEDED
1	BACK BOARD	$5/8 \times 9 \times 14^{1}/_{2}$	1
2	SIDE	$5/8 \times 5^{1}/_{2} \times 7$	2
3	BOTTOM	$^{1}/_{2} \times 5^{1}/_{2} \times 9$	1
4	FRONT BOARD	$5/8 \times 3^{3}/_{8} \times 10^{1}/_{4}$	1

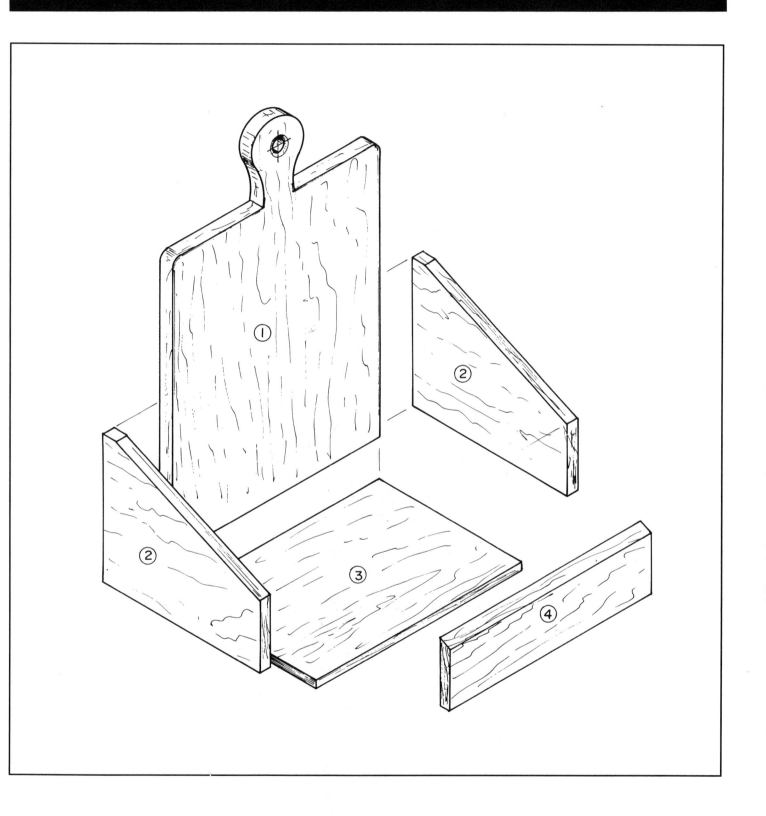

Wall Box

This candle box was painted green and trimmed with yellow. Dimensions are 5½ inches deep by 11 inches wide by 16½ inches high.

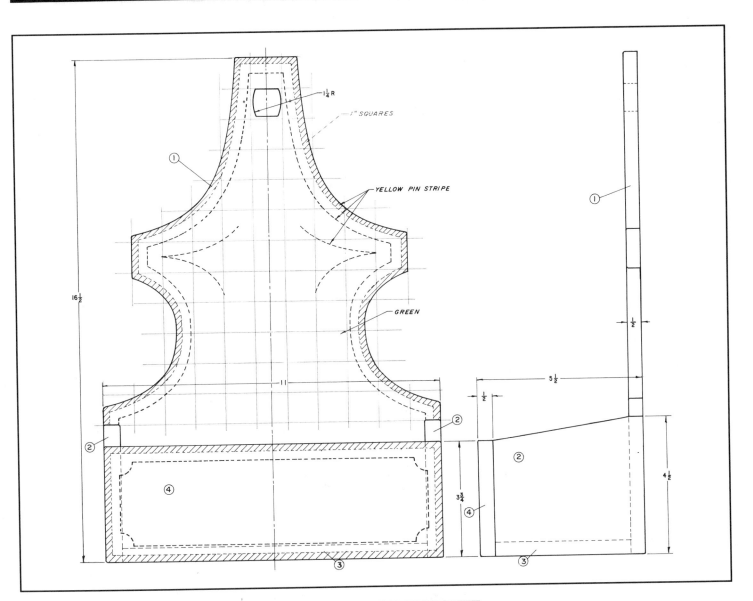

PART	INCHES	NEEDED
1 BACK BOARD	$1/2 \times 11 \times 16^{1}/2$	1
2 SIDES	$1/2 \times 4^{1}/2 \times 5^{1}/2$	2
3 BOTTOM	$1/2 \times 4^{1}/2 \times 10$	1
4 FRONT	$1/2 \times 3^{3}/4 \times 11$	1

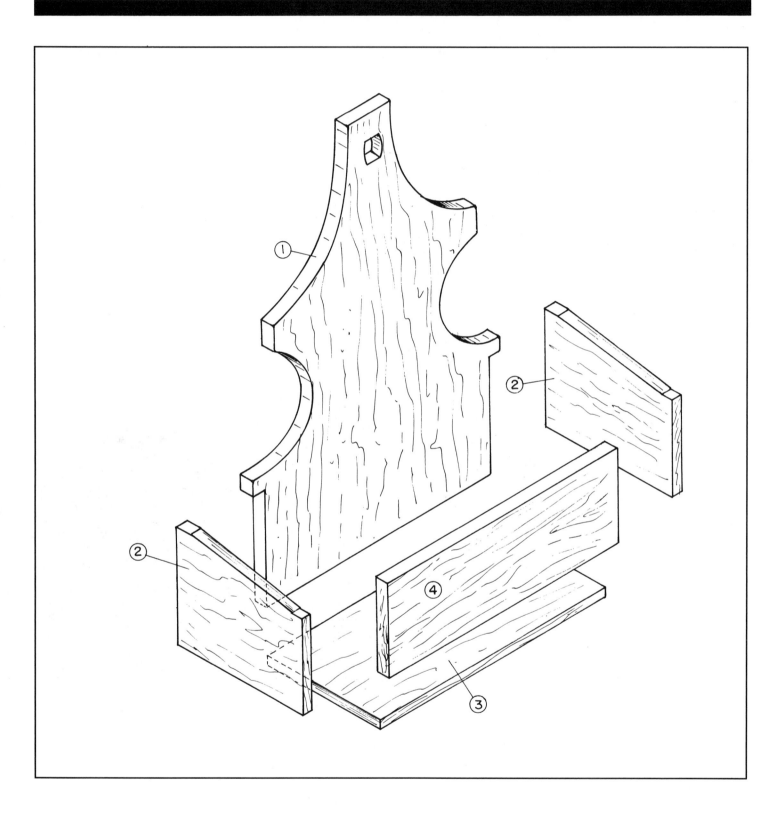

Candle Box

Many early candle boxes used this basic design and construction. The original of the box shown here was made of pine and then painted. It had many wear marks and was found in northern New England. Measurements are 5 inches deep by 12³/₄ inches wide by 8³/₄ inches high.

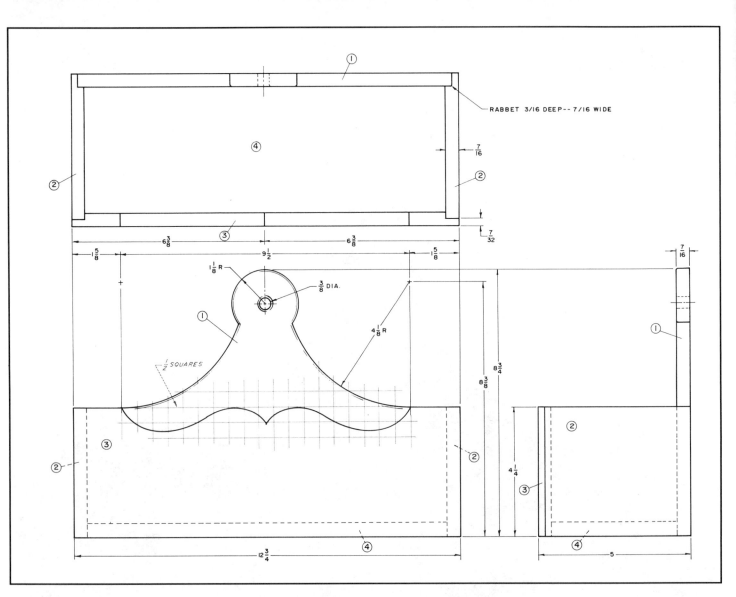

RABBET 3/16 DEEP-- 7/16 WIDE

PART	INCHES	NEEDED
1 BACK BOARD	$7/16 \times 8^5/16 \times 12^5/16$	1
2 SIDE	$7/16 \times 4^1/4 \times 4^{13}/16$	2
3 FRONT	$7/16 \times 4^1/4 \times 12^3/4$	1
4 BOTTOM	$7/16 \times 4^1/8 \times 11^7/8$	1

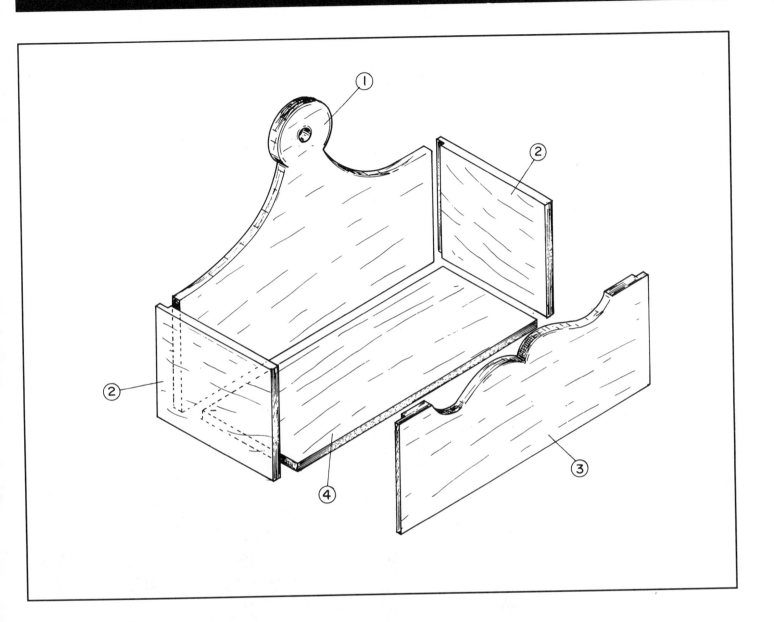

Two-Tiered Candle Box

The original of the box shown here, made around 1815, was of pine, painted moss green. It measures 4 inches deep by 11½ inches wide by 14½ inches high.

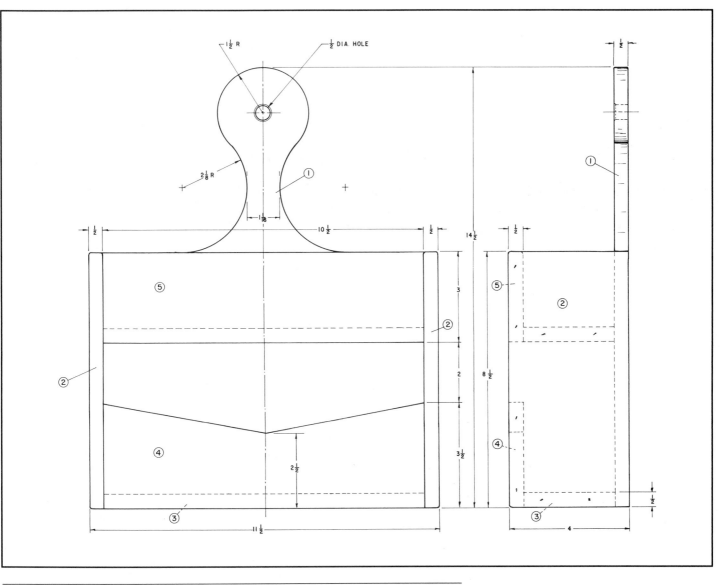

PART	INCHES	NEEDED
1 BACK BOARD	$1/2 \times 10^{1}/2 \times 14^{1}/2$	1
2 SIDE	$1/2 \times 4 \times 8^{1}/2$	2
3 BOTTOM	$1/2 \times 3 \times 10^{1}/2$	2
4 FRONT BOTTOM	$1/2 \times 3^{1}/2 \times 10^{1}/2$	1
5 FRONT TOP	$1/2 \times 3 \times 10^{1}/2$	1

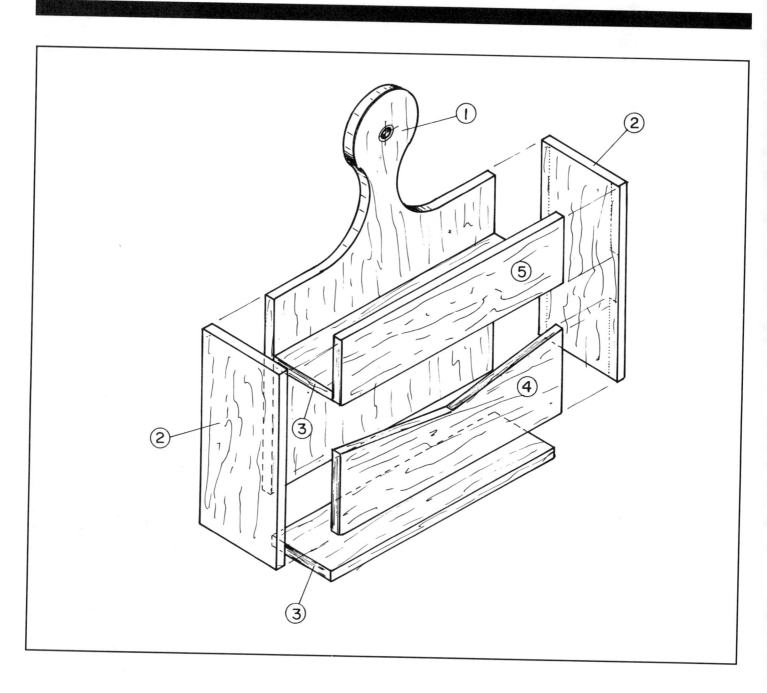

Fishtail Candle Box

This wall-hanging box is modeled after one made in Pennsylvania around 1800. The original was painted gray-green and measures 4¹/₂ inches deep by 12 inches wide by 5¹/₄ inches high.

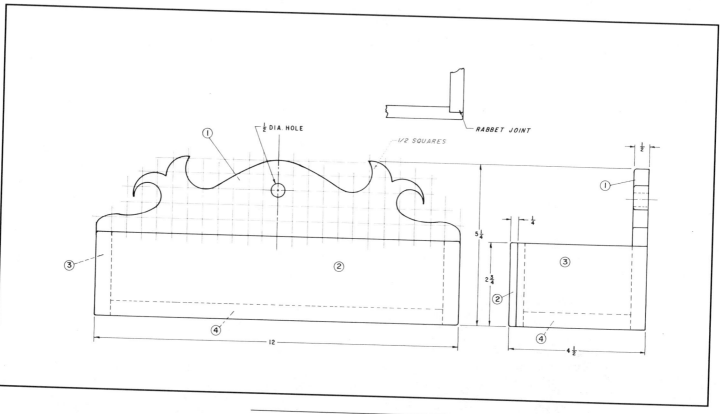

PART		INCHES	NEEDED
1	BACK BOARD	1/2 × 5 1/4 × 12	1
2	FRONT	1/2 × 2 3/4 × 12	1
3	SIDE	1/2 × 2 3/4 × 4 1/4	2
4	BOTTOM	1/2 × 3 1/2 × 11	1

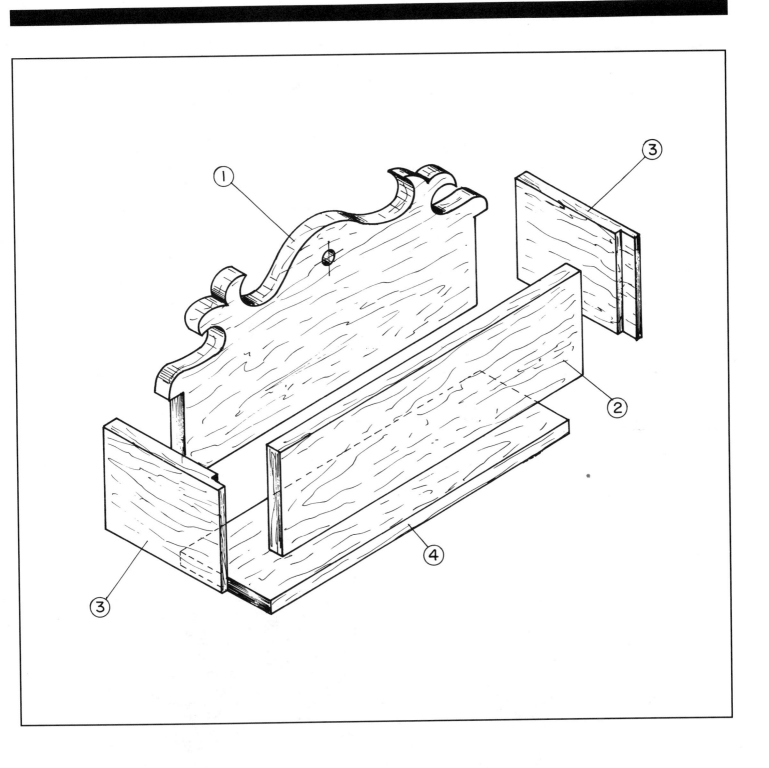

WALL BOXES

Early crafters made all kinds of wall boxes: large, small, with shelves, with drawers, very plain, highly decorated. They held spices, candles, salt, clay pipes, tobacco, tea, or whatever else the colonial housewife chose to store.

In its early, simplest form, the wall box was just a box hung on the wall without a lid. In later years the lid, drawers, and shelves were added. As new needs arose and the makers tried more complicated designs, more and more drawers were added. Nails were no longer sufficient to attach these heavier boxes to the wall, and soon they were made to stand on other furniture or on the floor.

Wall boxes were made with butt joints, rabbet joints, and sometimes dovetail joints. They were held together by handmade square-cut nails. No attempt was made to conceal these nails, and the heads can be seen. For an authentic look, use old, used square-cut nails and round the box's edges and corners.

Early Wall Box

The original had a crinkle varnish finish and was said to have been made in 1760. Found in Francestown, New Hampshire, it is hardwood and has simple lines. Dimensions are 5 1/2 inches deep by 12 9/16 inches wide by 9 1/8 inches high.

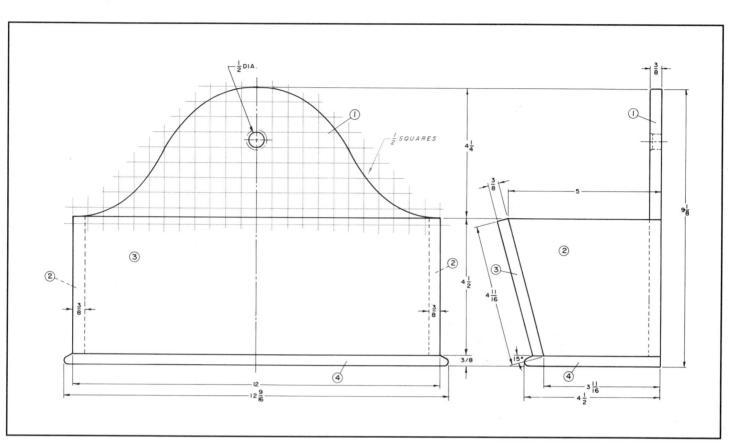

PART	INCHES	NEEDED
1 BACK BOARD	$3/8 \times 8^3/4 \times 11^1/4$	1
2 SIDE	$3/8 \times 4^1/2 \times 5$	2
3 FRONT BOARD	$3/8 \times 4^{11}/16 \times 12$	1
4 BASE	$3/8 \times 4^1/2 \times 12^9/16$	1

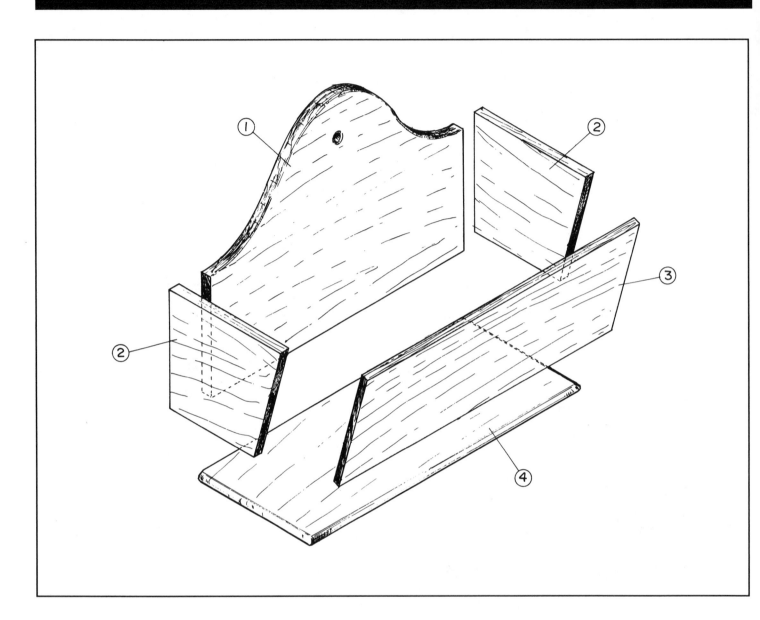

Primitive Wall Box

This wall box may have been used in a barn to hold chicken grain. The original was found in Massachusetts. It measures 4¹/₂ inches deep by 8 inches wide by 16 inches high.

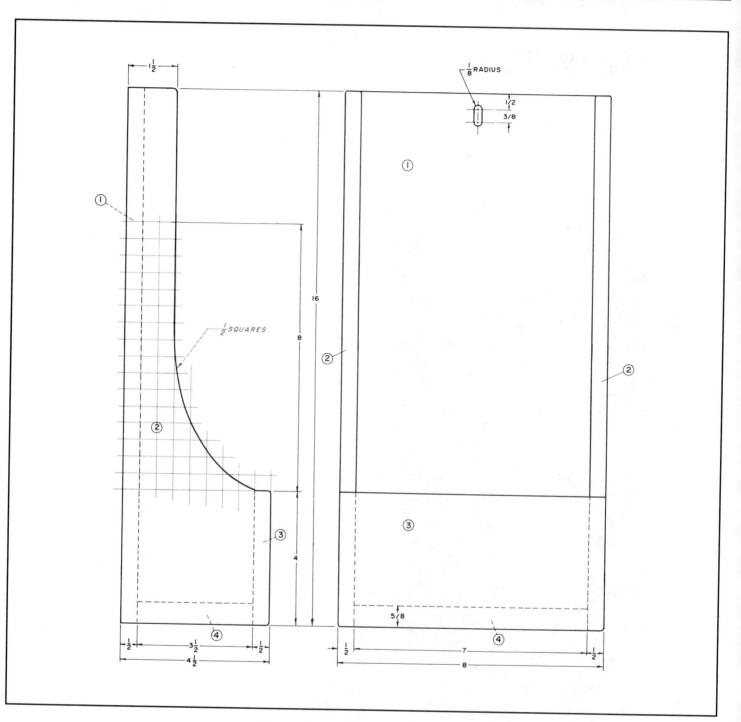

PART	INCHES	NEEDED
1 BACK BOARD	$\frac{1}{2} \times 7 \times 16$	1
2 SIDE	$\frac{1}{2} \times 4\frac{1}{2} \times 16$	2
3 FRONT	$\frac{1}{2} \times 4 \times 8$	1
4 BOTTOM	$\frac{1}{2} \times 3\frac{1}{2} \times 7$	1

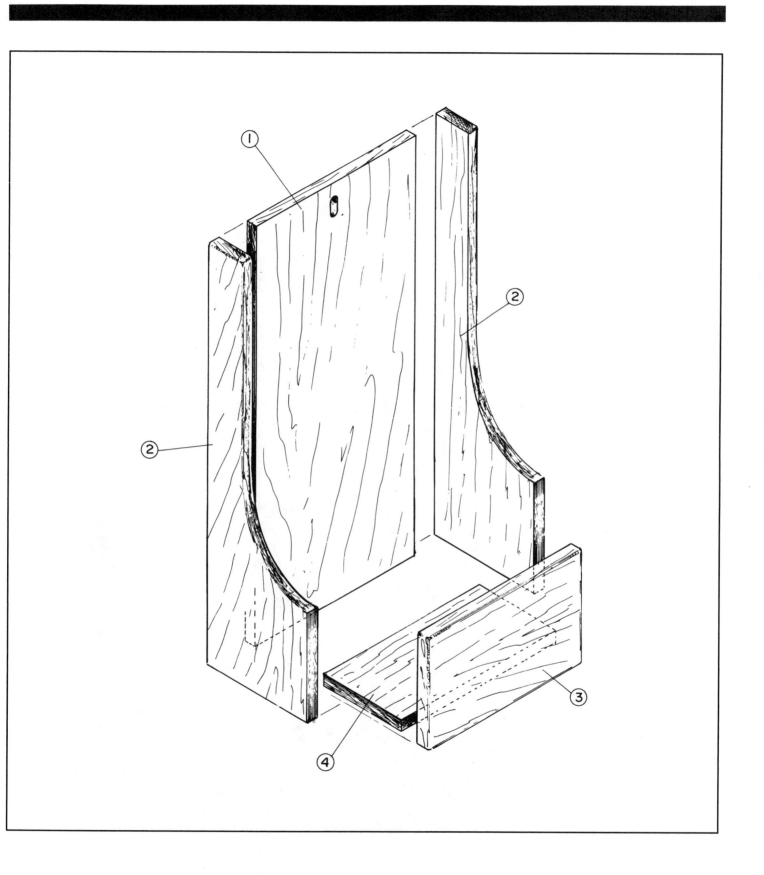

Country Wall Box

Nice, simple lines characterize this 1800 wall box. The original was painted powder blue on pine. Of unknown origin, it measures 6 inches deep by 7⅞ inches wide by 12½ inches high.

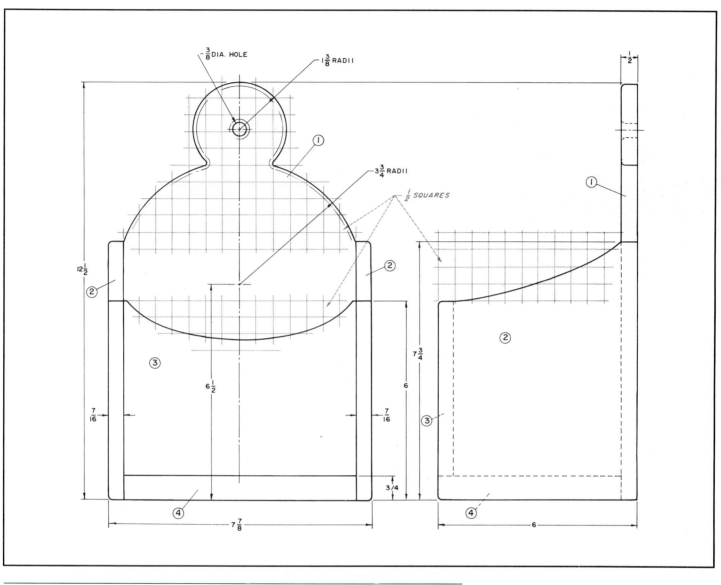

PART	INCHES	NEEDED
1 BACK BOARD	$1/2 \times 7 \times 12^1/2$	1
2 SIDE	$7/16 \times 6 \times 7^3/4$	2
3 FRONT	$7/16 \times 7 \times 5^1/4$	1
4 BOTTOM	$3/4 \times 5^1/2 \times 7$	1

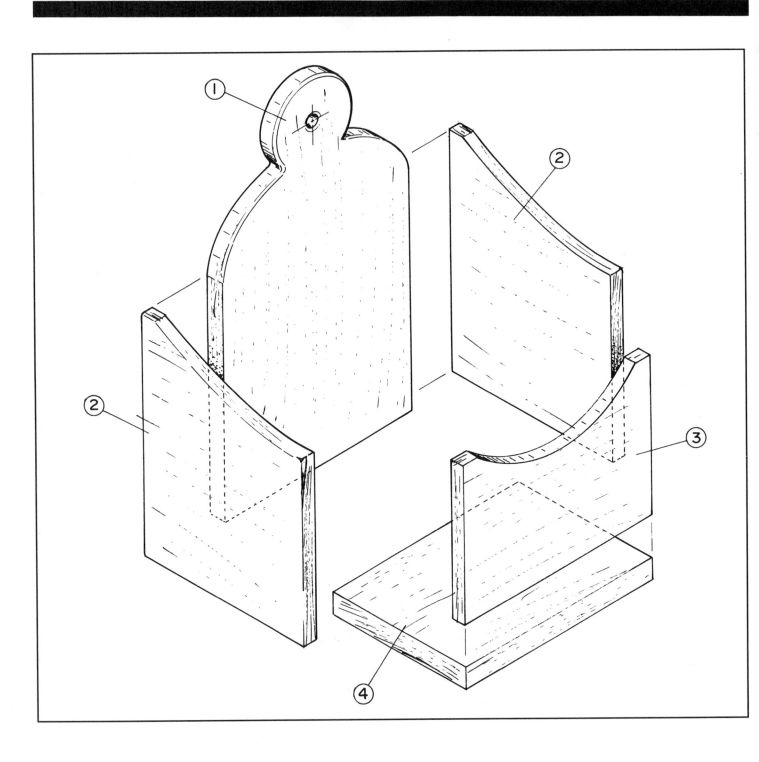

Small Formal Wall Box

Made of mahogany around 1850, this small box has a sophisticated design. Its origin is unknown. Dimensions are 3 3/4 inches deep by 8 1/2 inches wide by 9 1/2 inches high.

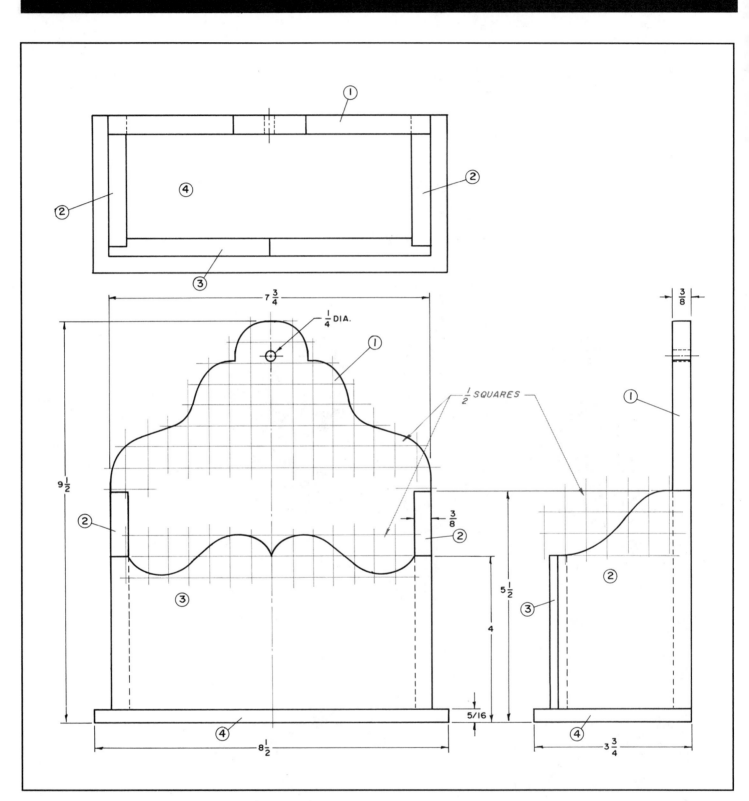

PART	INCHES	NEEDED
1 BACK BOARD	$3/8 \times 7^3/4 \times 9^3/16$	1
2 SIDE	$3/8 \times 3^3/16 \times 5^3/16$	2
3 FRONT	$3/8 \times 4^3/16 \times 7^3/4$	1
4 BOTTOM	$5/16 \times 3^3/4 \times 8^1/2$	1

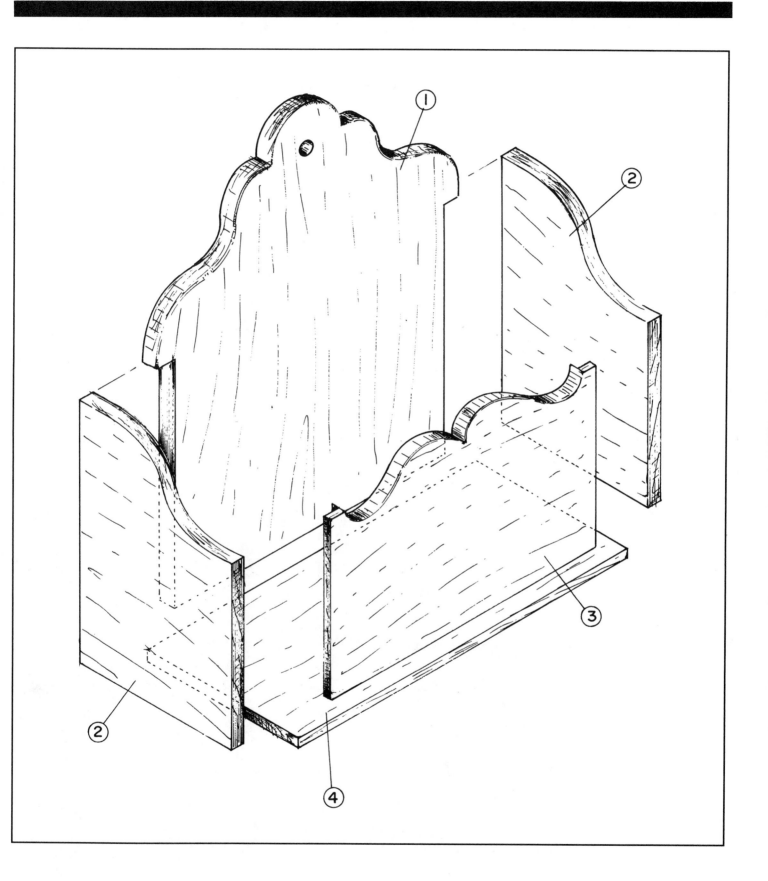

Hanging Country Wall Box

Of a particularly attractive design, the original was pine painted gray. It was made around 1775 and found in New England. Dimensions are 5 inches deep by 10½ inches wide by 12 inches high.

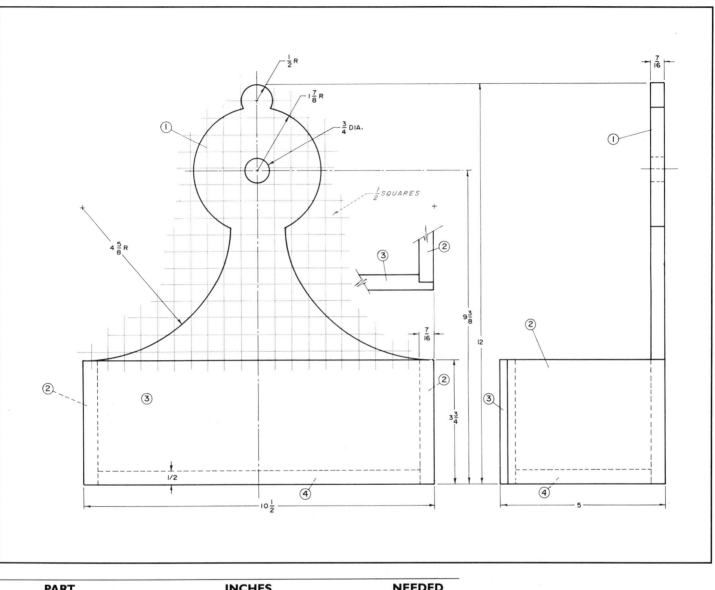

PART	INCHES	NEEDED
1 BACK BOARD	$7/16 \times 9^{5}/_{8} \times 12$	1
2 SIDE	$7/16 \times 3^{3}/_{4} \times 4^{3}/_{4}$	2
3 FRONT	$7/16 \times 3^{3}/_{4} \times 10^{1}/_{2}$	1
4 BOTTOM	$7/16 \times 4^{1}/_{8} \times 9^{5}/_{8}$	1

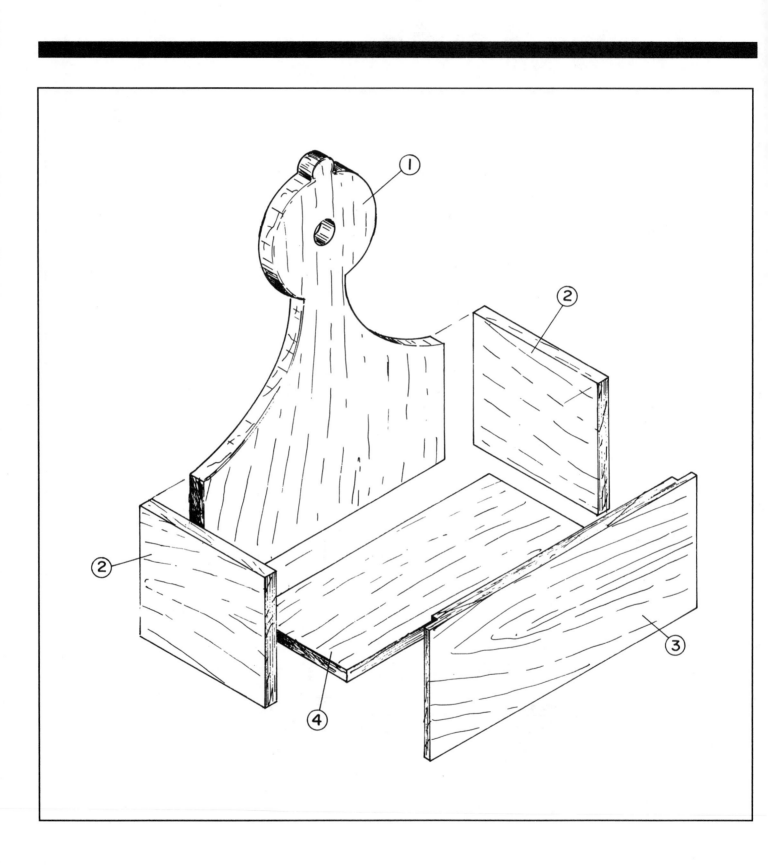

Formal Wall Box

The original of this box was made around 1700 of birch. It features raked sides, a corn finial, and dovetailed construction. Its origin is unknown. Measurements are 4^1/$_2$ inches deep by 11 inches wide by 13^1/$_4$ inches high.

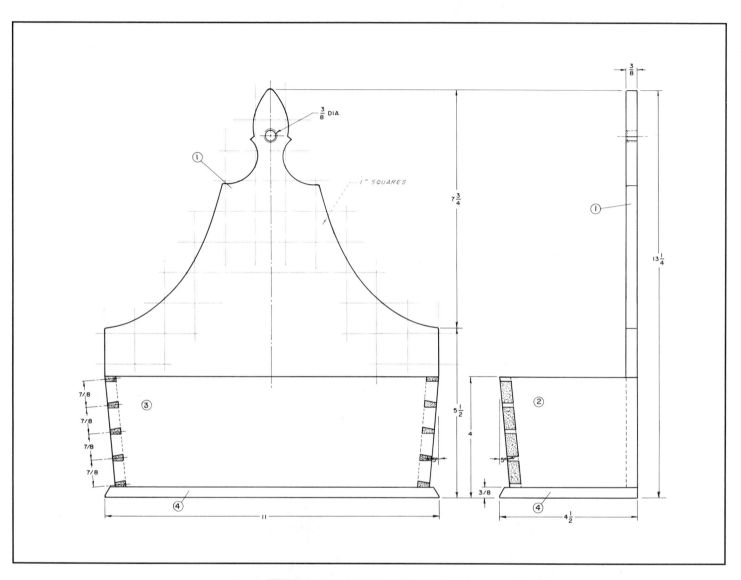

$\frac{3}{8}$ DIA.

1" SQUARES

$7\frac{3}{4}$

$5\frac{1}{2}$

4

$\frac{3}{8}$

7/8

7/8

7/8

7/8

11

$\frac{3}{8}$

$13\frac{1}{4}$

$4\frac{1}{2}$

5°

PART	INCHES	NEEDED
1 BACK BOARD	$\frac{3}{8} \times 11 \times 12\frac{7}{8}$	1
2 SIDE	$\frac{3}{8} \times 3\frac{5}{8} \times 4\frac{1}{2}$	2
3 FRONT	$\frac{3}{8} \times 3\frac{5}{8} \times 11$	1
4 BOTTOM	$\frac{3}{8} \times 4\frac{1}{2} \times 11$	1

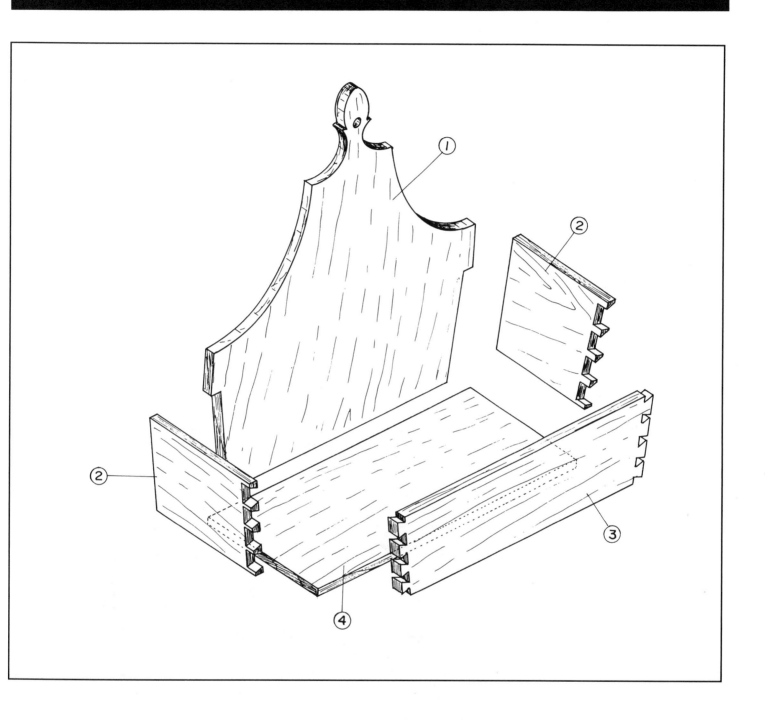

Large Wall Box

The box shown is painted pine and has a unique design. Its origin is unknown. Dimensions are 5 inches deep by 10 inches wide by 15 inches high.

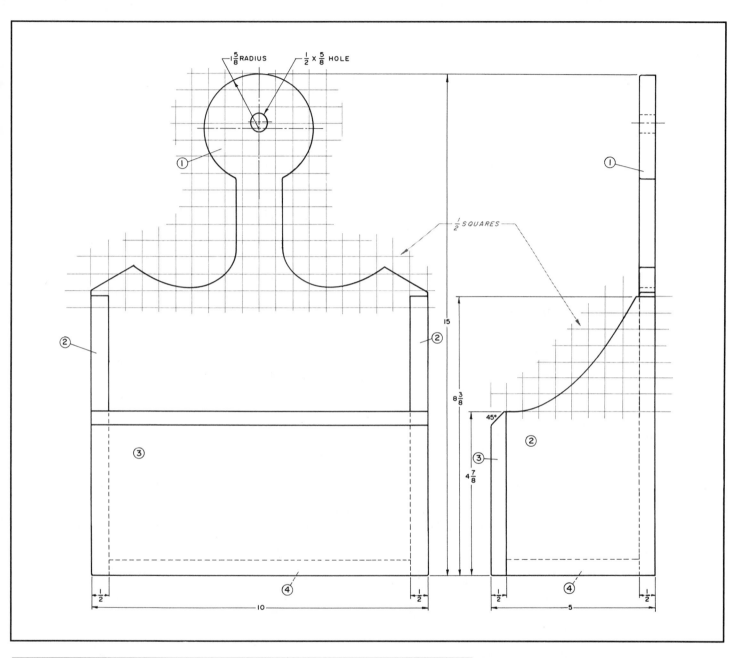

PART	INCHES	NEEDED
1 BACK BOARD	$1/2 \times 10 \times 15$	1
2 SIDE	$1/2 \times 4 \times 8^{3/8}$	2
3 FRONT	$1/2 \times 4^{7/8} \times 10$	1
4 BOTTOM	$1/2 \times 4 \times 9$	1

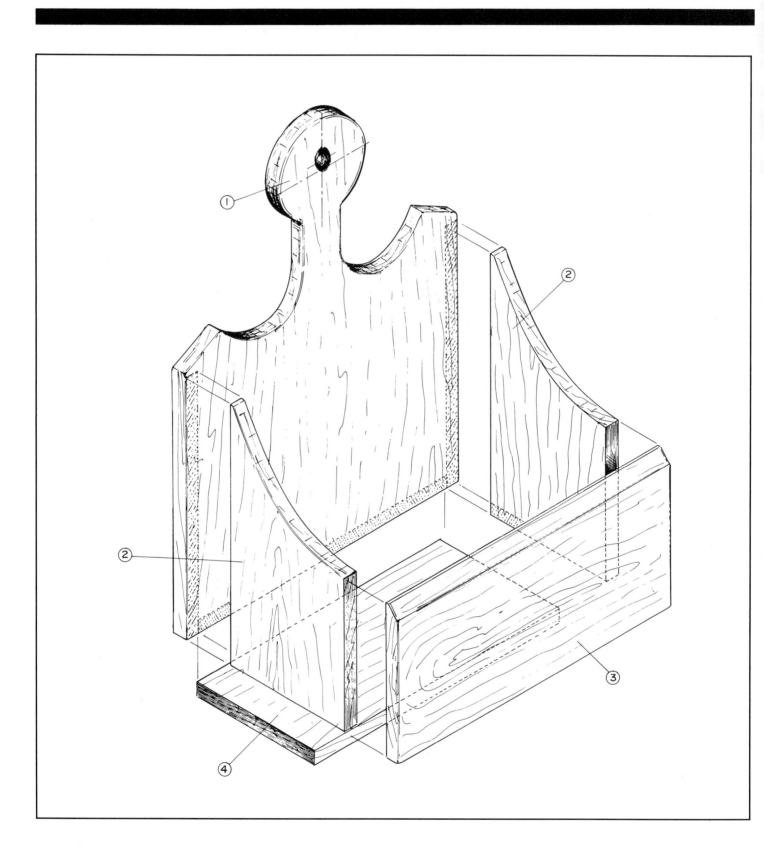

Pine Wall Box

The original of this hanging wall box, made around 1825, was painted black. It measures 4¹/₄ inches deep by 7 inches wide by 22 inches high.

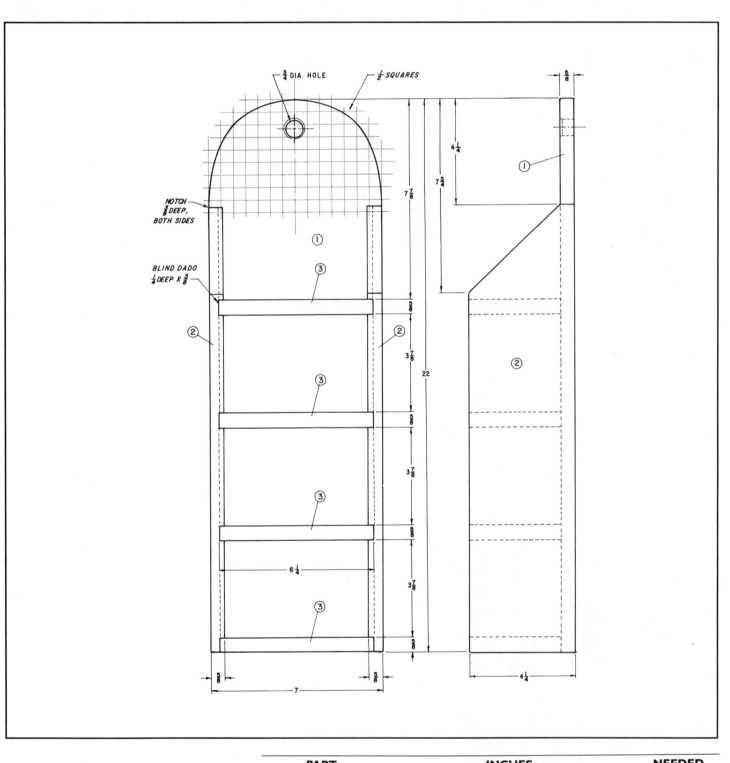

PART	INCHES	NEEDED
1 BACK BOARD	⅝ × 7 × 22	1
2 SIDE	⅝ × 4¼ × 17¾	2
3 SHELF	⅝ × 3⅝ × 6¼	4

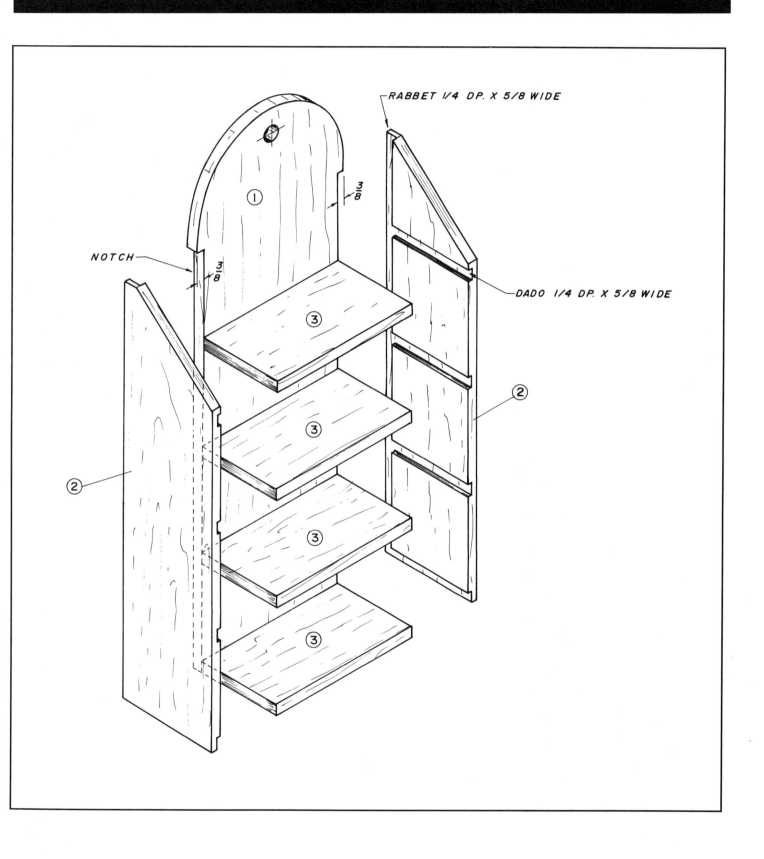

RABBET 1/4 DP. X 5/8 WIDE

① ③⁄₈

NOTCH ③⁄₈

② ③ ③ ③ ③

② DADO 1/4 DP. X 5/8 WIDE

Tool-Sharpening Wall Box

It is said that sand was stored in the bottom of this unusual wall box; when its owner wanted to sharpen a knife or tool, he would wet the sand, dip the blade into it, then rub the blade up and down on the leather belt. True or not, this will surely be a conversation piece. The original, made of pine, was found in Hancock, New Hampshire. It measures 4 3/4 inches deep by 5 1/2 inches wide by 36 inches high.

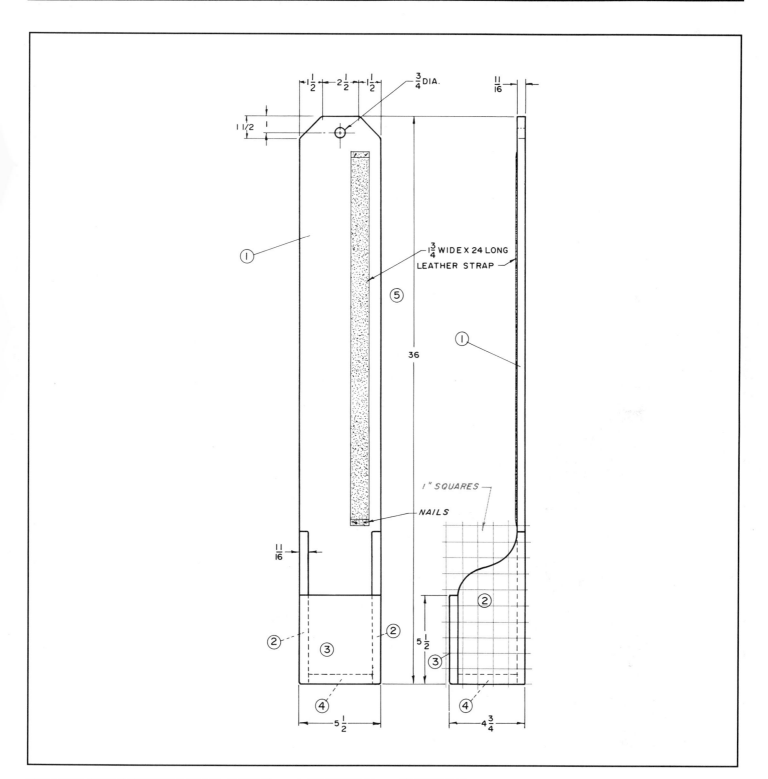

PART	INCHES	NEEDED
1 BACK BOARD	$^{11}/_{16} \times 5^{1}/_{2} \times 36$	1
2 SIDE	$^{11}/_{16} \times 4^{1}/_{16} \times 9^{3}/_{4}$	2
3 FRONT	$^{11}/_{16} \times 5^{1}/_{2} \times 5^{1}/_{2}$	1
4 BOTTOM	$^{11}/_{16} \times 3^{3}/_{8} \times 4^{1}/_{8}$	1
5 LEATHER STRAP	$^{1}/_{8} \times 1^{3}/_{4} \times 24$	1

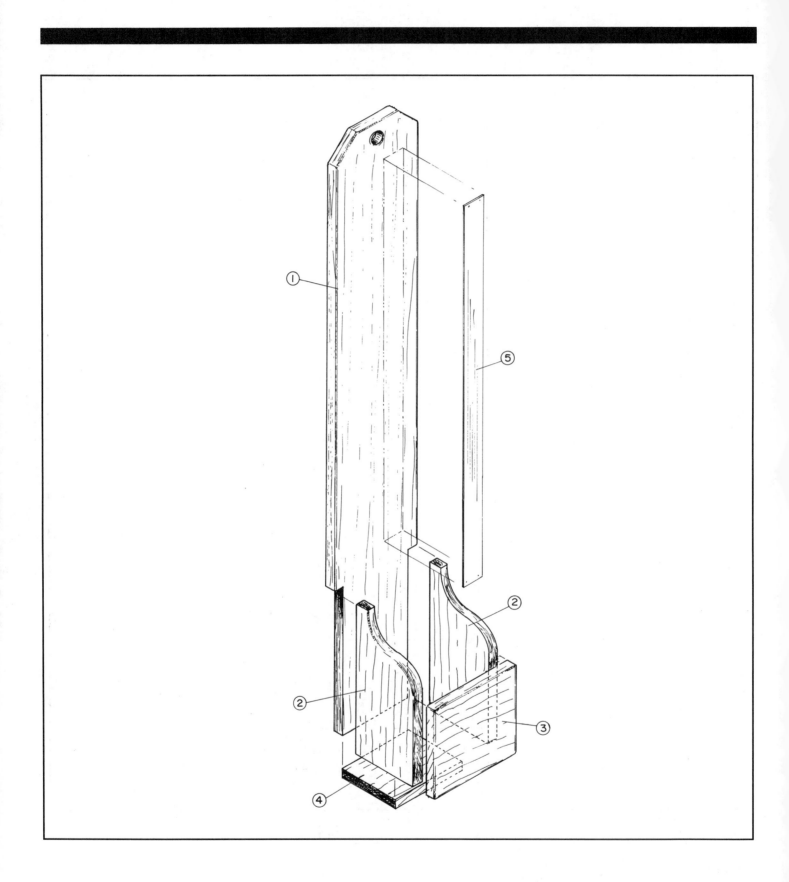

Whaler's Scrimshaw Box

This wall-hanging box has a lid and compartments for tools. The original was made of walnut around 1850 and featured brass hinges. Located in Rhode Island, it had arched grooves and worn marks from swinging back and forth on a whaling ship for many years. It measures $4^1/_2$ inches deep by $9^5/_8$ inches wide by $10^1/_2$ inches high.

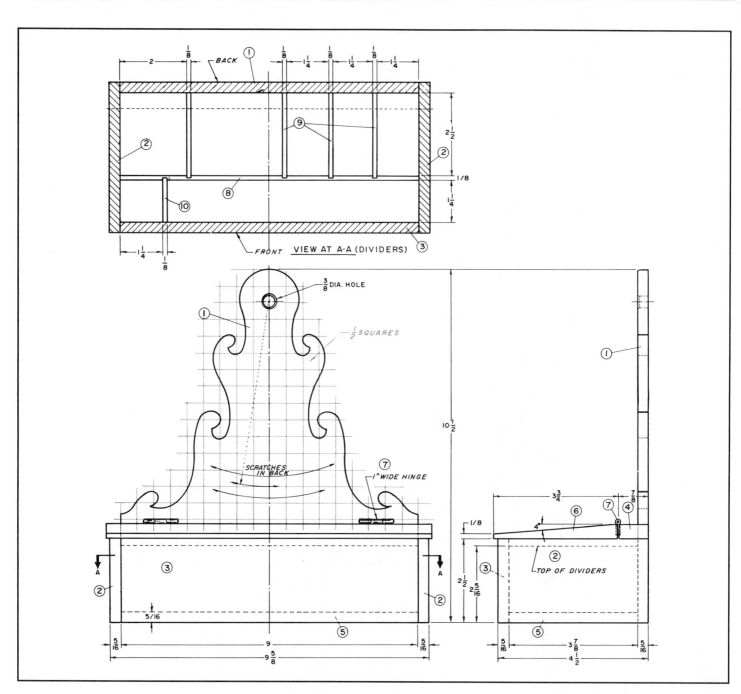

VIEW AT A-A (DIVIDERS)

$\frac{3}{8}$ DIA. HOLE

$\frac{1}{2}$ SQUARES

SCRATCHES IN BACK

1" WIDE HINGE

TOP OF DIVIDERS

	PART	INCHES	NEEDED
1	BACK	$5/16 \times 9 \times 10^{1}/_{2}$	1
2	SIDE	$5/16 \times 2^{1}/_{2} \times 4^{1}/_{2}$	2
3	FRONT	$5/16 \times 2^{1}/_{2} \times 9$	1
4	TOP	$7/16 \times 7/8 \times 9^{7}/_{8}$	1
5	BOTTOM	$5/16 \times 3^{7}/_{8} \times 9$	1
6	LID	$7/16 \times 3^{3}/_{4} \times 9^{7}/_{8}$	1
7	BRASS HINGE	1×1	2
8	DIVIDER	$1/8 \times 2^{5}/_{16} \times 9$	1
9	DIVIDER	$1/8 \times 2^{5}/_{16} \times 2^{9}/_{16}$	4
10	DIVIDER	$1/8 \times 2^{5}/_{16} \times 1^{5}/_{16}$	1

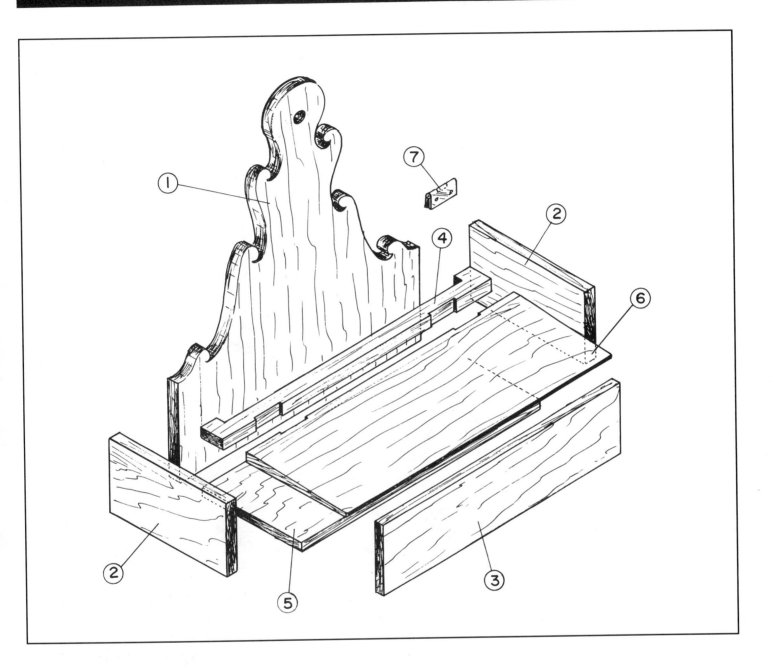

Salt Box with Lid

Of hardwood, the original of this box was painted brown. It was found in Massachusetts. Measurements are 6 inches deep by 10½ inches wide by 13¾ inches high.

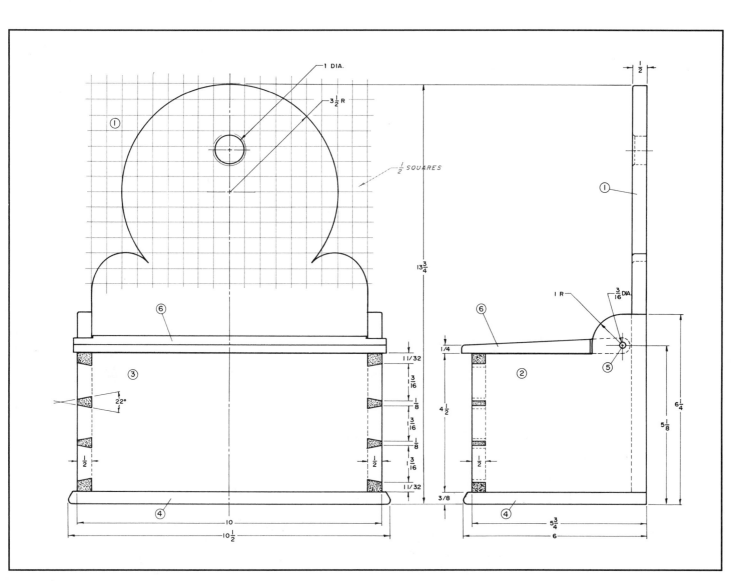

PART		INCHES	NEEDED
1	BACK	$1/2 \times 9 \times 13^3/8$	1
2	SIDE	$1/2 \times 5^3/4 \times 6^1/4$	2
3	FRONT	$1/2 \times 4^1/2 \times 10$	1
4	BOTTOM	$3/8 \times 6 \times 10^1/2$	1
5	PIN	$3/16$ DIAMETER $\times 1$	2

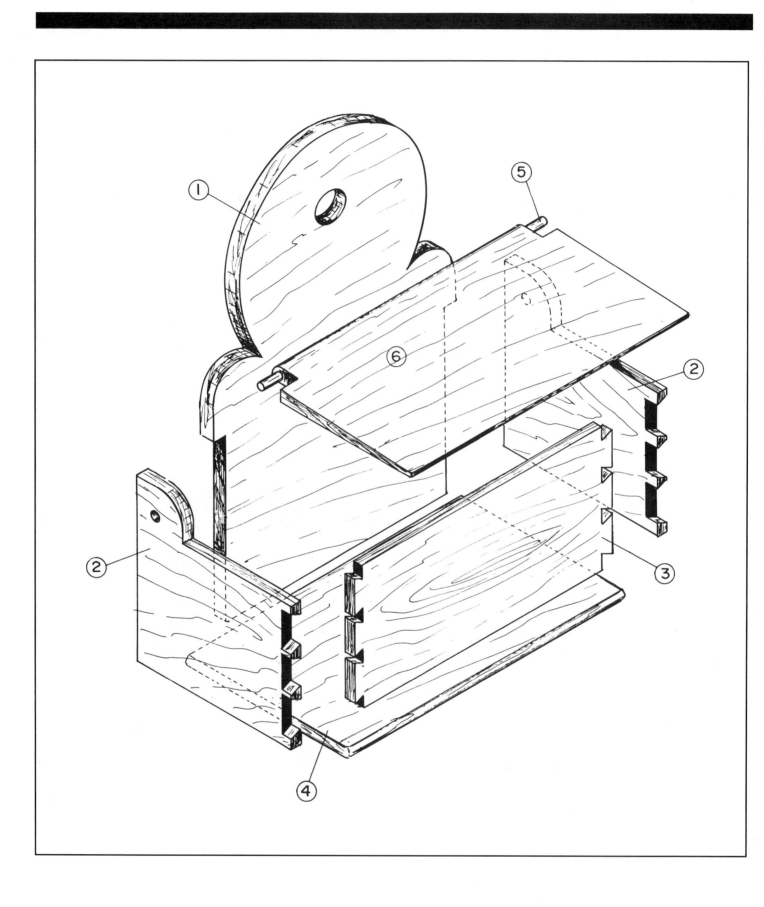

Formal Box with Lid and Drawer

The original was of hardwood, painted red, from Pennsylvania. Note that the drawer front is flush with the sides. Dimensions are $6^5/_{16}$ inches deep by $11^7/_8$ inches wide by $11^3/_4$ inches high.

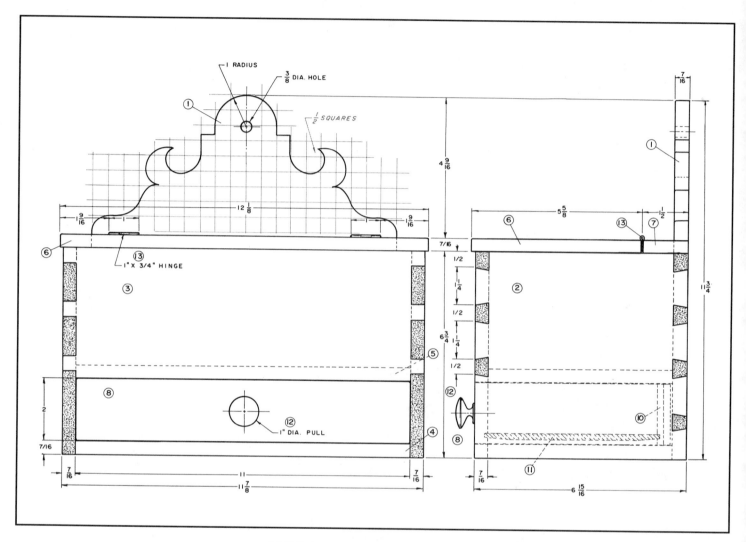

PART		INCHES	NEEDED
1	BACK	$7/16 \times 11^3/4 \times 11^7/8$	1
2	SIDE	$7/16 \times 6^3/4 \times 6^{15}/16$	2
3	FRONT	$7/16 \times 4^5/16 \times 11^7/8$	1
4	BOTTOM	$7/16 \times 6^1/2 \times 11$	1
5	SHELF	$7/16 \times 6^1/16 \times 11$	1
6	LID	$7/16 \times 5^5/8 \times 12^1/8$	1
7	SUPPORT	$7/16 \times 1^1/2 \times 12^1/8$	1
8	DRAWER FRONT	$1/2 \times 2 \times 11$	1
9	DRAWER SIDE	$1/4 \times 2 \times 6^1/16$	2
10	DRAWER BACK	$1/4 \times 2 \times 10^3/4$	1
11	DRAWER BOTTOM	$1/4 \times 5^3/4 \times 10^3/4$	1
12	WOODEN PULL	1 DIAMETER	1
13	BRASS HINGE	$1 \times 3/4$	2

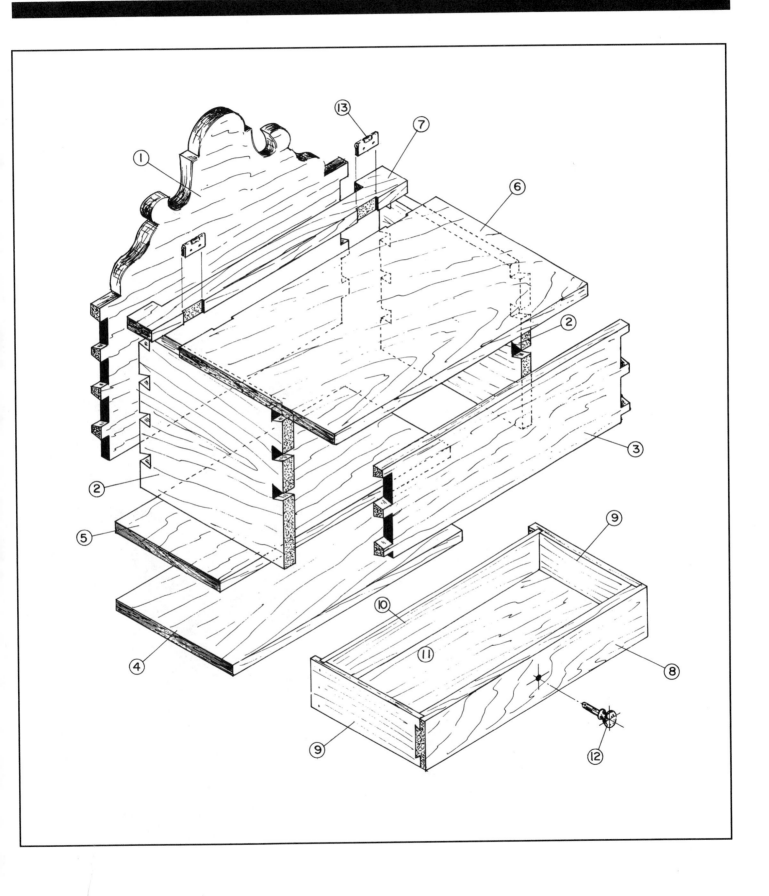

Country Salt Box

This box, definitely country in style, has a lid and a drawer of the overlapping type. It measures 7^{15}/$_{16}$ inches deep by 11^7/$_8$ inches wide by 13 inches high.

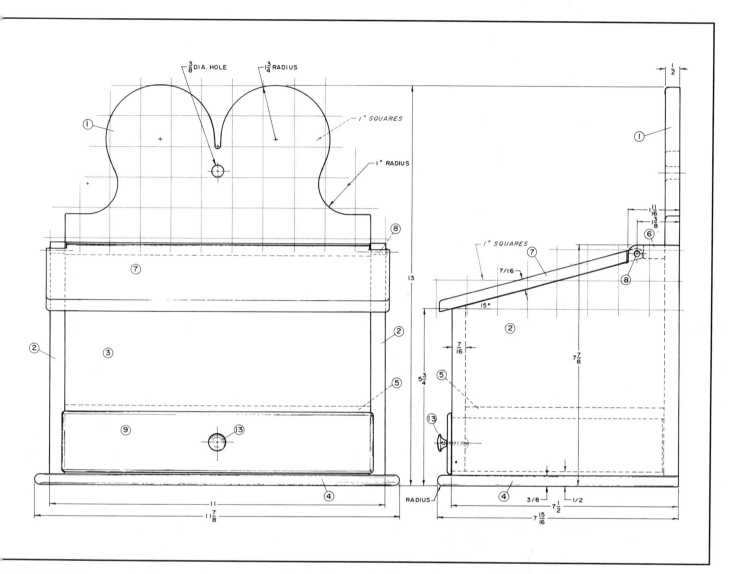

PART		INCHES	NEEDED
1	BACK	$1/2 \times 10 \times 12^{5}/_8$	1
2	SIDE	$1/2 \times 7^{1}/_2 \times 7^{1}/_2$	2
3	FRONT	$7/_{16} \times 3^{3}/_4 \times 10$	1
4	BOTTOM	$1/2 \times 7^{15}/_{16} \times 11^{7}/_8$	1
5	DIVIDER	$3/8 \times 6^{9}/_{16} \times 10$	1
6	SUPPORT	$1/2 \times {}^{11}/_{16} \times 10$	1
7	LID	$7/_{16} \times 6^{9}/_{16} \times 11^{1}/_4$	1
8	PIN	$3/_{16}$ DIAMETER $\times 1$	2
9	DRAWER FRONT	$1/2 \times 2 \times 10^{1}/_4$	1
10	DRAWER SIDE	$1/4 \times 1^{3}/_4 \times 6^{3}/_4$	2
11	DRAWER BACK	$1/4 \times 1^{3}/_4 \times 9^{3}/_4$	1
12	DRAWER BOTTOM	$1/4 \times 6^{3}/_8 \times 9^{3}/_4$	1
13	WOODEN PULL	$5/8$ DIAMETER	1

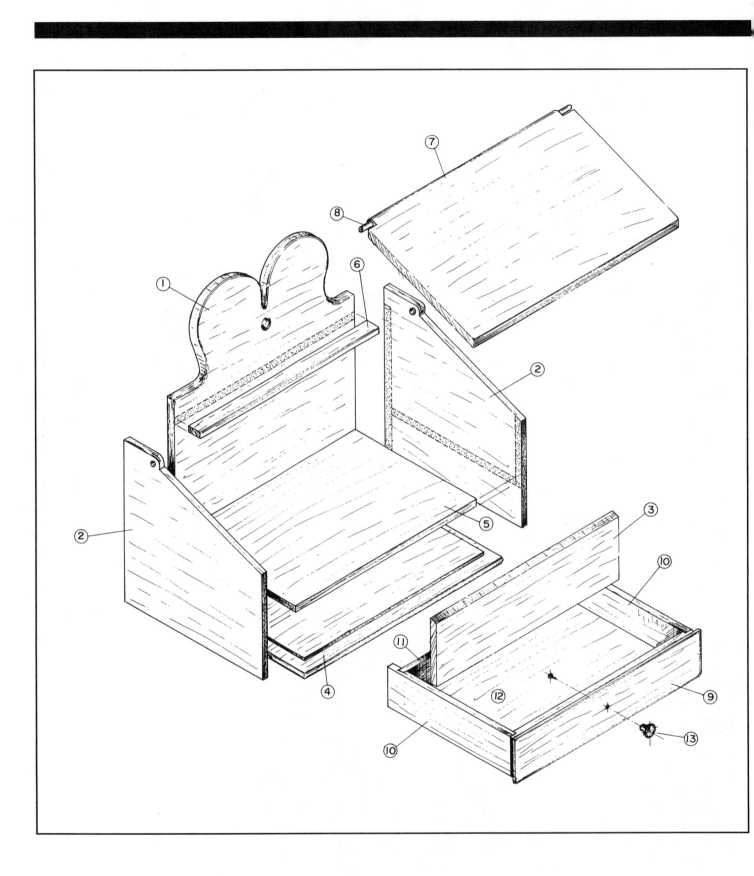

Open Box with Drawer

This hanging wall box is of unfinished pine. The original came from Nova Scotia. It measures 6½ inches deep by 10⅞ inches wide by 17 inches high.

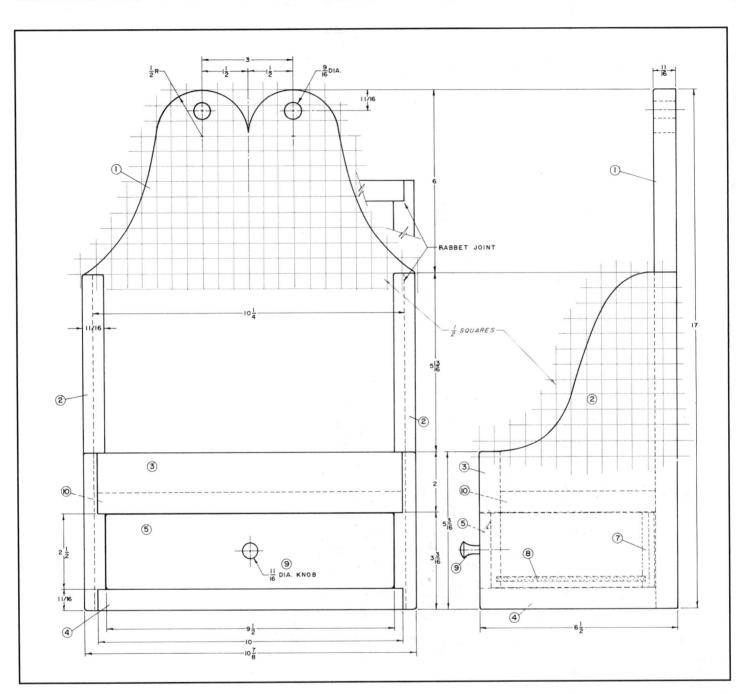

PART		INCHES	NEEDED
1	BACK	$^{11}/_{16} \times 10^{7}/_{8} \times 17$	1
2	SIDE	$^{11}/_{16} \times 6^{1}/_{2} \times 11$	2
3	FRONT	$^{11}/_{16} \times 2 \times 10$	1
4	BOTTOM	$^{11}/_{16} \times 5^{13}/_{16} \times 10$	1
5	DRAWER FRONT	$^{11}/_{16} \times 2^{1}/_{2} \times 9^{1}/_{2}$	1
6	DRAWER SIDE	$^{1}/_{4} \times 2^{1}/_{2} \times 5^{3}/_{8}$	2
7	DRAWER BACK	$^{1}/_{4} \times 2^{1}/_{2} \times 9^{1}/_{4}$	1
8	DRAWER BOTTOM	$^{1}/_{8} \times 4^{7}/_{8} \times 9^{1}/_{4}$	1
9	WOODEN KNOB	$^{11}/_{16}$ DIAMETER	1
10	SHELF	$^{11}/_{16} \times 5^{1}/_{8} \times 10$	1

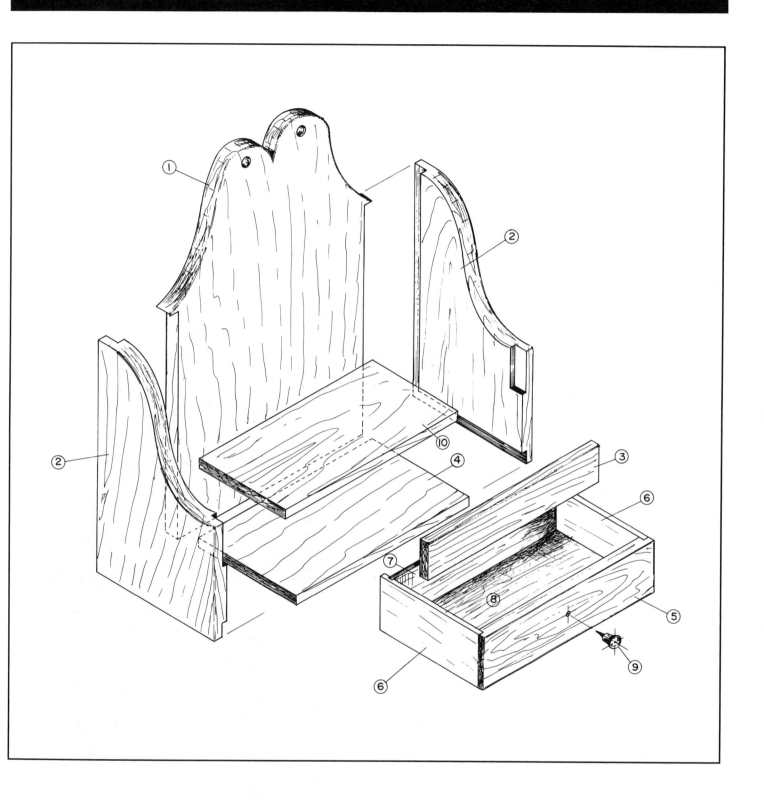

Formal Salt Box

Note the wood-hinged lid. Made of mahogany, the original was found in New London, New Hampshire. Its dimensions are 5³/4 inches deep by 8¹/2 inches wide by 11¹/4 inches high.

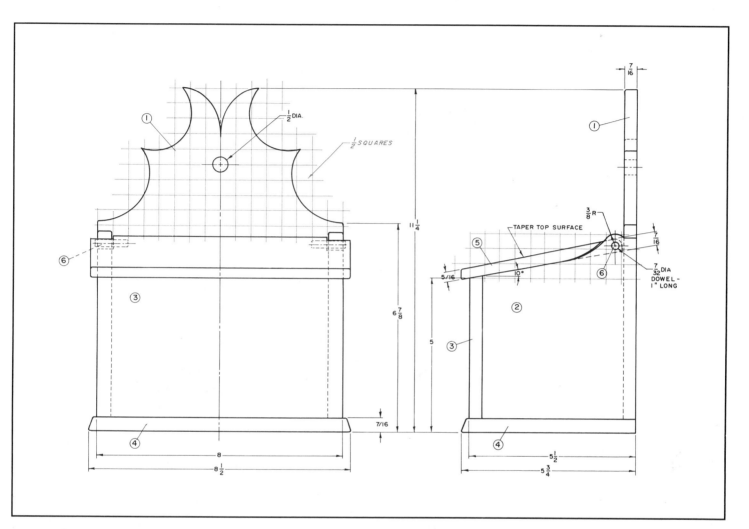

PART	INCHES	NEEDED
1 BACK	$^{7}/_{16}$ × 8 × 10$^{13}/_{16}$	1
2 SIDE	$^{7}/_{16}$ × 5$^{1}/_{16}$ × 6$^{1}/_{16}$	2
3 FRONT	$^{7}/_{16}$ × 4$^{3}/_{4}$ × 8	1
4 BOTTOM	$^{7}/_{16}$ × 5$^{3}/_{4}$ × 8$^{1}/_{2}$	1
5 LID	$^{7}/_{16}$ × 5$^{1}/_{2}$ × 8$^{1}/_{2}$	1
6 PIN	$^{7}/_{32}$ DIAMETER × 1$^{1}/_{8}$	2

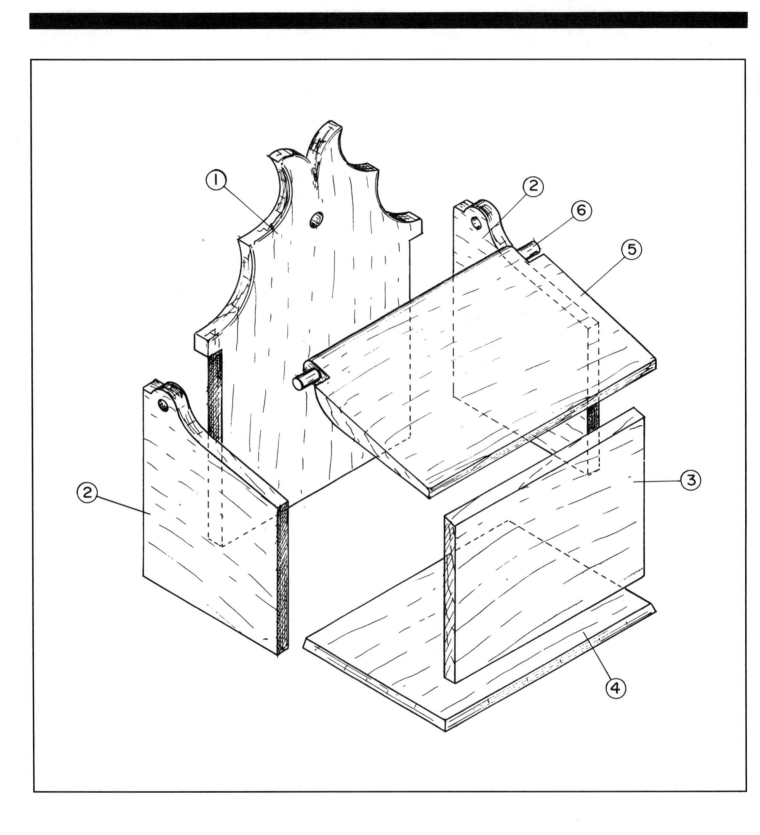

MIRROR

Glass for mirrors was very expensive and scarce in early days. Some very early mirrors were made of pieces of broken glass attached to a frame.

A courting mirror was a common present given to a young woman by a hopeful beau during his courtship. It was said that if the girl smiled into the mirror after he proposed, she would surely accept.

Courting Mirror

This Chippendale-style mirror features two upside-down hearts and a stylized tulip on top. The dentil molding is a classic pattern of its day, and the early swastika is an ancient design that signified good luck. The mirror measures 8½ by 18 inches.

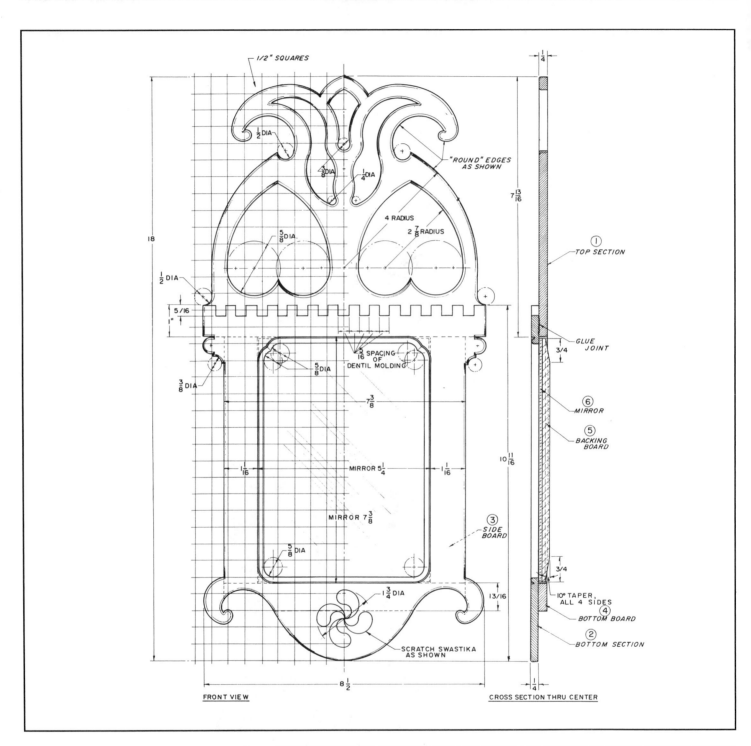

	PART	INCHES	NEEDED
1	TOP SECTION	$1/4 \times 8^{1}/_{2} \times 7^{13}/_{16}$	1
2	BOTTOM SECTION	$1/4 \times 8^{1}/_{2} \times 10^{11}/_{16}$	1
3	SIDE BOARD	$1/4 \times 1 \times 7^{1}/_{2}$	2
4	BOTTOM BOARD	$1/4 \times {^{13}/_{16}} \times 7^{3}/_{8}$	1
5	BACK BOARD	$1/4 \times 5^{1}/_{4} \times 7^{3}/_{8}$	1
6	MIRROR	$3/32 \times 5^{1}/_{4} \times 7^{3}/_{8}$	1
7	FINISHED SQUARE-CUT NAIL	$3/4$	8

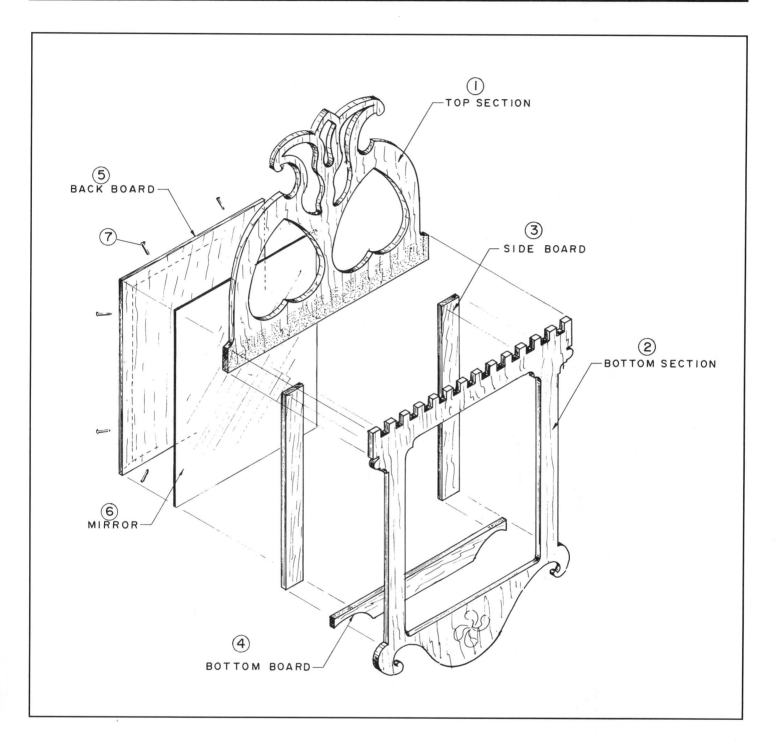

① TOP SECTION

⑤ BACK BOARD

⑦

③ SIDE BOARD

② BOTTOM SECTION

⑥ MIRROR

④ BOTTOM BOARD

PIPE BOXES

In years past, when men gathered around the fireplace to share one another's company, the clay pipe was usually brought out. Yet even in those days smoking was considered dangerous. King James I called it "a custom lothsome to the eye, hateful to the Nose, harmefull to the braine, daungerous to the Lungs, and in the blacke stinking fume thereof, neerest resembling the horrible Stigian smoke of the pit that is bottomelesse." Despite such warnings, the European settlers of the New World became addicted to tobacco. Over 2,500 pounds of it were consumed in this country in 1616, and by 1775 well over 100 million pounds. With the increased popularity of tobacco and pipe smoking there came a need for a special place to store the long-stemmed clay pipes—thus the birth of the pipe box. The pipes were stored in the open top area, and the drawer below held the tobacco.

Pipe boxes were popular from 1745 to around 1790. Although many were made, very few can be found today except in museums. No two pipe boxes were made exactly alike. They ranged from very formal boxes, beautifully and delicately made, to crude, heavy ones. Most were made of hardwood, 1/4 inch to 3/8 inch thick. Cherry, maple, mahogany, and walnut were the woods usually chosen, but pine was also sometimes used, especially on the more informal, country boxes.

Today you can use the pipe box to store envelopes and stamps or candles and matches. It also makes a great planter. However you use it, a pipe box can add the warmth of yesterday to any room.

Hancock Pipe Box

A very unusual design. The original of this box was found in Hancock, New Hampshire. It was made of poplar around 1850. Dimensions are 4⁷/8 inches deep by 4¹/4 inches wide by 22³/4 inches high.

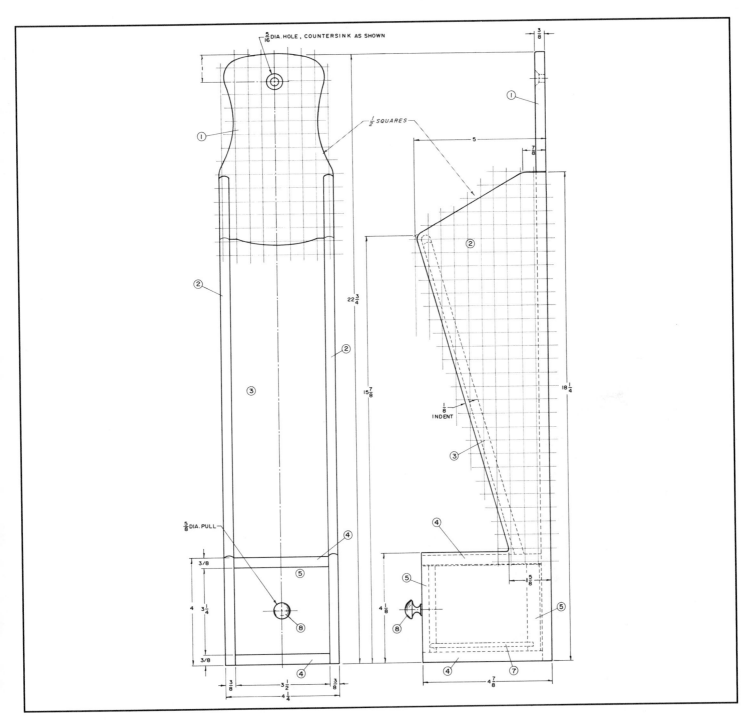

PART		INCHES	NEEDED
I	BACK	$3/8 \times 4^{1}/4 \times 22^{3}/4$	I
2	SIDE	$3/8 \times 5 \times 18^{1}/4$	2
3	FRONT	$3/8 \times 3^{1}/2 \times 12^{1}/2$	I
4	DIVIDER	$3/8 \times 4^{1}/2 \times 3^{1}/2$	2
5	DRAWER FRONT / BACK	$1/2 \times 3^{1}/4 \times 3^{1}/2$	2
6	DRAWER SIDE	$1/4 \times 3^{1}/4 \times 4^{1}/4$	2
7	DRAWER BOTTOM	$1/8 \times 3^{1}/4 \times 3^{7}/8$	I
8	WOODEN PULL	$5/8$ DIAMETER	I

167

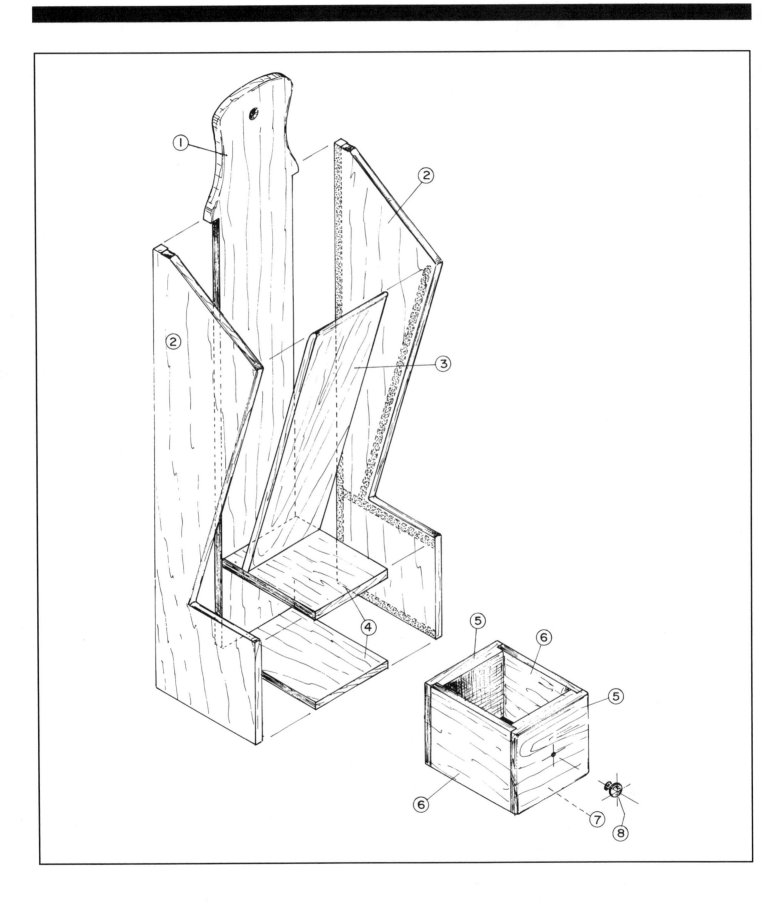

Pine Pipe Box

Made of pine, this box has a drawer for the tobacco. The original was found in Massachusetts. It measures 4½ inches deep by 6 inches wide by 16 inches high.

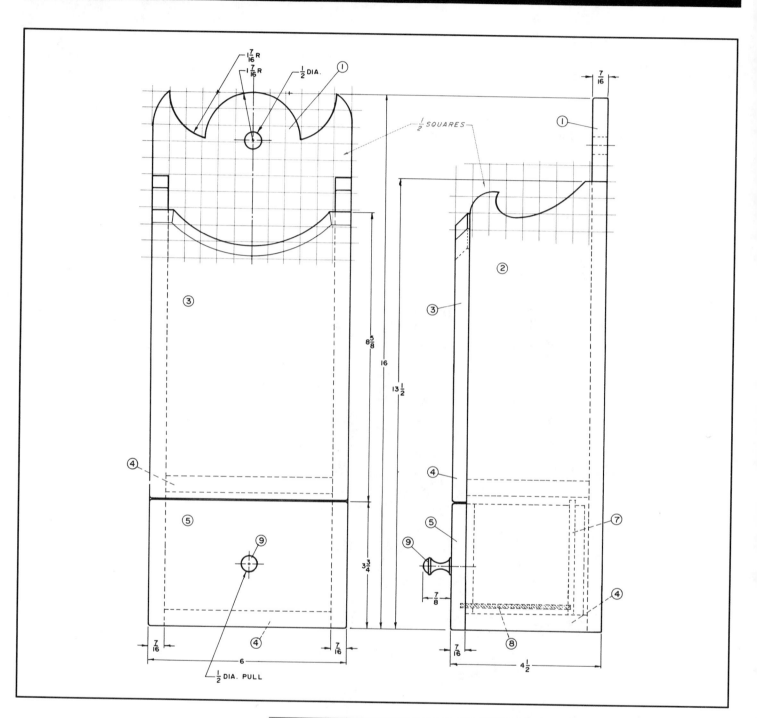

PART	INCHES	NEEDED
1 BACK	$7/16 \times 6 \times 16$	1
2 SIDE	$7/16 \times 4^{1}/16 \times 13^{1}/2$	2
3 FRONT	$7/16 \times 6 \times 8^{5}/8$	1
4 DIVIDER	$7/16 \times 3^{5}/8 \times 5^{1}/8$	2
5 DRAWER FRONT	$11/16 \times 3^{3}/4 \times 6$	1
6 DRAWER SIDE	$1/4 \times 3^{3}/4 \times 3^{5}/8$	2
7 DRAWER BACK	$1/4 \times 3^{3}/4 \times 4^{7}/8$	1
8 DRAWER BOTTOM	$1/8 \times 3^{1}/4 \times 4^{7}/8$	1
9 WOODEN PULL	$1/2$ DIAMETER	1

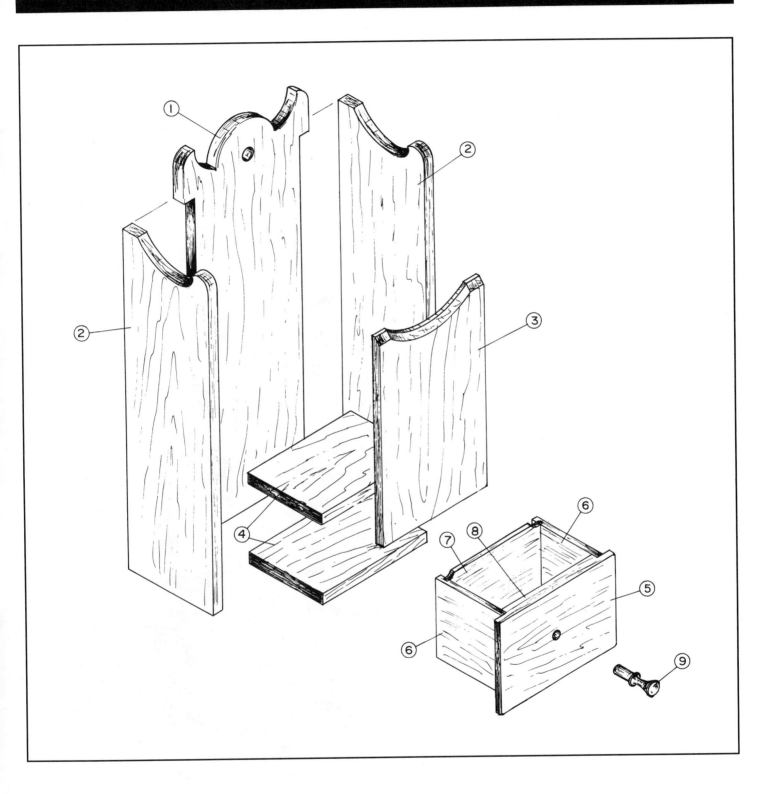

Provincetown Pipe Box

Of heavy, solid, dovetail construction, the original of this box was made around 1800. It was found on Cape Cod, at Provincetown. It measures 5³/4 inches deep by 7 inches wide by 16 inches high.

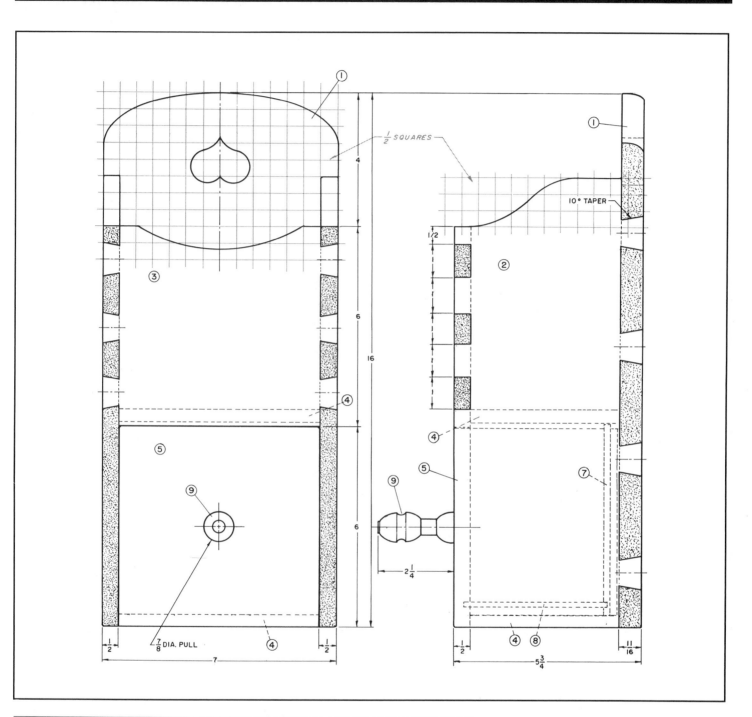

PART		INCHES	NEEDED
1	BACK	$^{11}/_{16} \times 7 \times 16$	1
2	SIDE	$^{1}/_{2} \times 5^{3}/_{4} \times 13^{1}/_{2}$	2
3	FRONT	$^{1}/_{2} \times 6 \times 7$	1
4	DIVIDER	$^{3}/_{8} \times 4^{9}/_{16} \times 6$	2
5	DRAWER FRONT	$^{1}/_{2} \times 6 \times 6$	1
6	DRAWER SIDE	$^{5}/_{16} \times 5^{1}/_{2} \times 4^{11}/_{16}$	2
7	DRAWER BACK	$^{5}/_{16} \times 5^{1}/_{2} \times 5^{5}/_{8}$	1
8	DRAWER BOTTOM	$^{1}/_{8} \times 4^{3}/_{8} \times 5^{5}/_{8}$	1
9	WOODEN PULL	$^{7}/_{8}$ DIAMETER	1

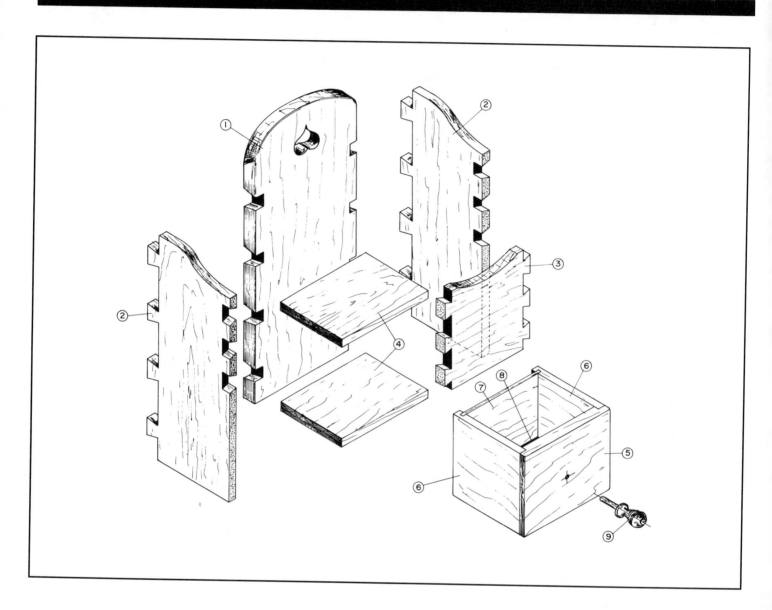

Castle Pipe Box

The castlelike edges set this country pipe box apart. The original, made of pine around 1800, was located at Sturbridge, Massachusetts. It measures 4⅝ inches deep by 6½ inches wide by 16 inches high.

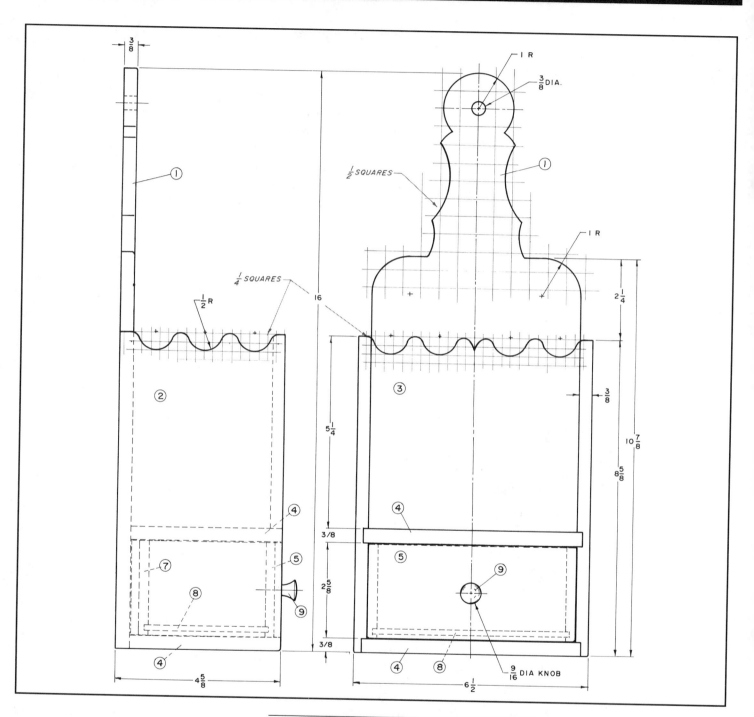

PART		INCHES	NEEDED
1	BACK	$3/8 \times 5^3/4 \times 16$	1
2	SIDE	$3/8 \times 4^5/8 \times 8^5/8$	2
3	FRONT	$3/8 \times 5^3/4 \times 5^1/4$	1
4	DIVIDER	$3/8 \times 4^1/4 \times 6^1/16$	2
5	DRAWER FRONT	$1/2 \times 2^5/8 \times 5^3/4$	1
6	DRAWER SIDE	$1/4 \times 2^5/8 \times 4$	2
7	DRAWER BACK	$1/4 \times 2^5/8 \times 5^1/2$	1
8	DRAWER BOTTOM	$1/8 \times 3^1/2 \times 5^1/2$	1
9	WOODEN PULL	$9/16$ DIAMETER	1

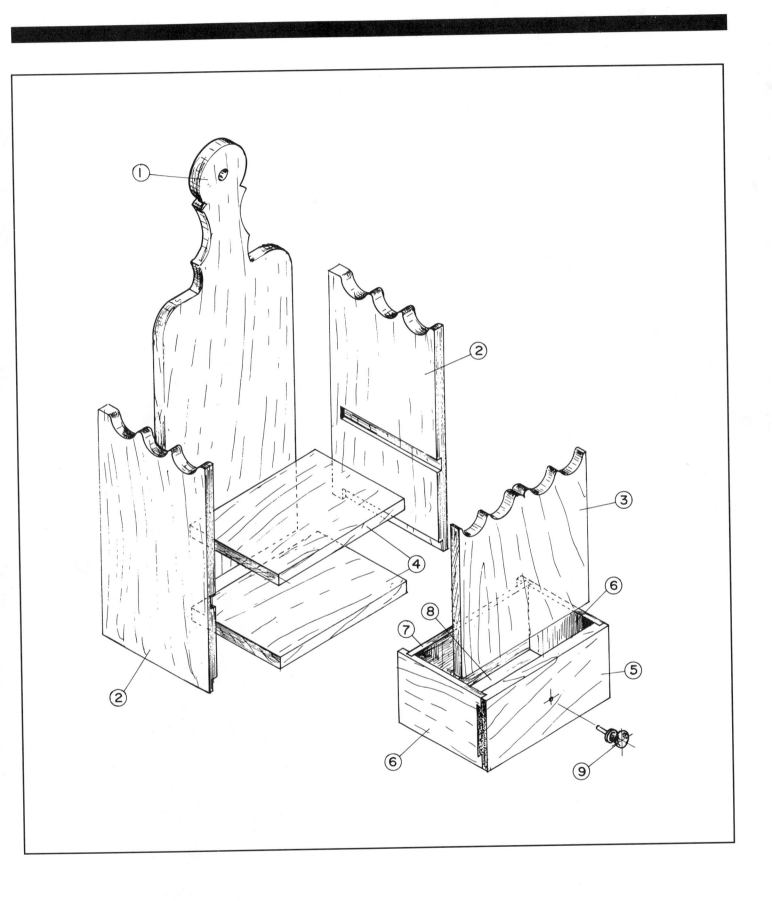

Country Pipe Box

Of an early design, this pipe box lacks the customary drawer. The original, whose provenance is unknown, was painted reddish brown on pine and has a compass-scratched design. A very primitive example. It measures 3³/₄ inches deep by 5 inches wide by 13¹/₂ inches high.

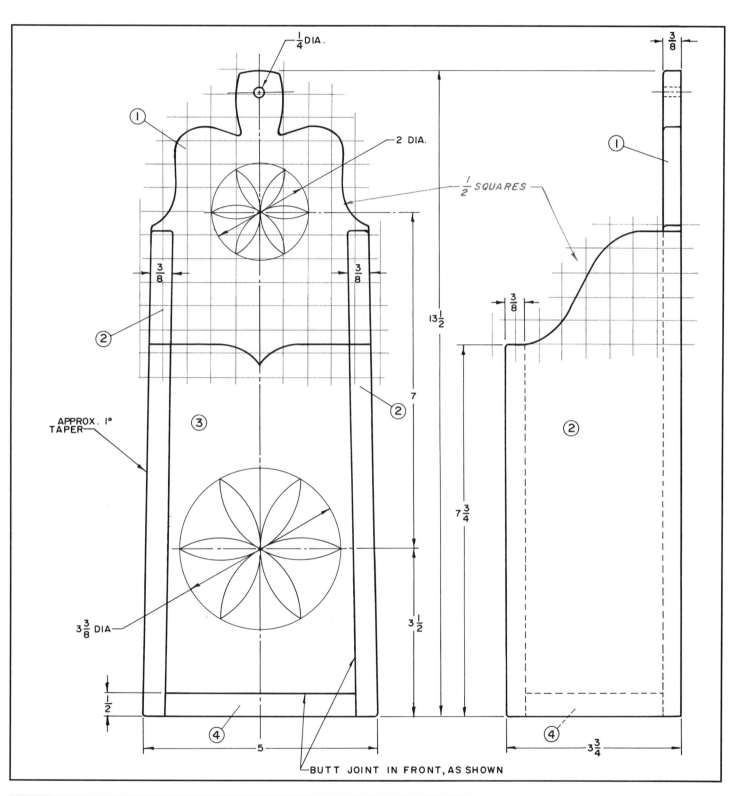

	PART	INCHES	NEEDED
I	BACK	3/8 × 4 1/4 × 13 1/2	I
2	SIDE	3/8 × 3 3/4 × 10 1/8	2
3	FRONT	3/8 × 4 1/4 × 7 1/4	I
4	BOTTOM	1/2 × 3 × 4 1/8	I

179

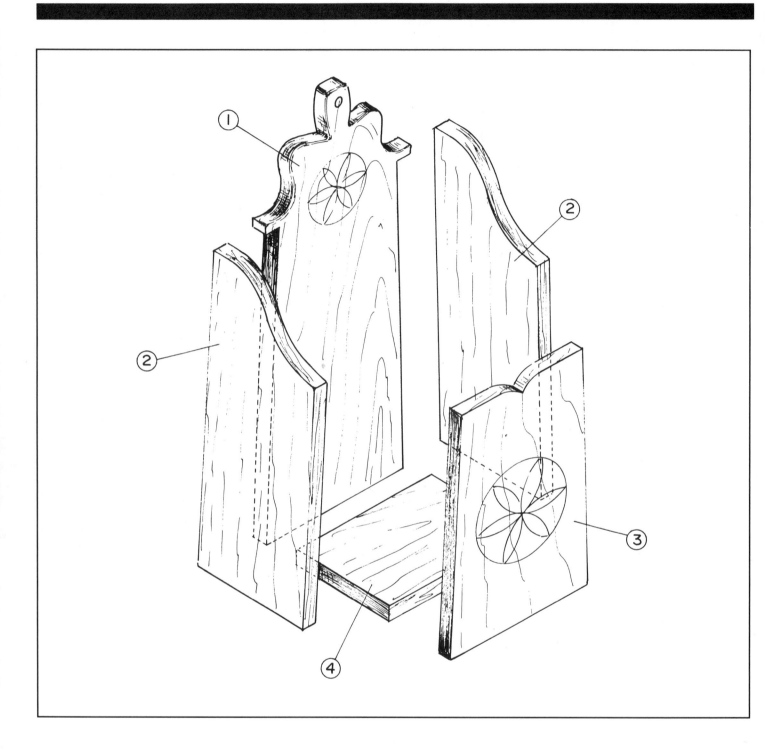

Two-Tiered Pipe Box

The original box was made of walnut around 1775. It is from Falmouth, Massachusetts. Dimensions are 6 inches deep by 6 3/4 inches wide by 24 inches high.

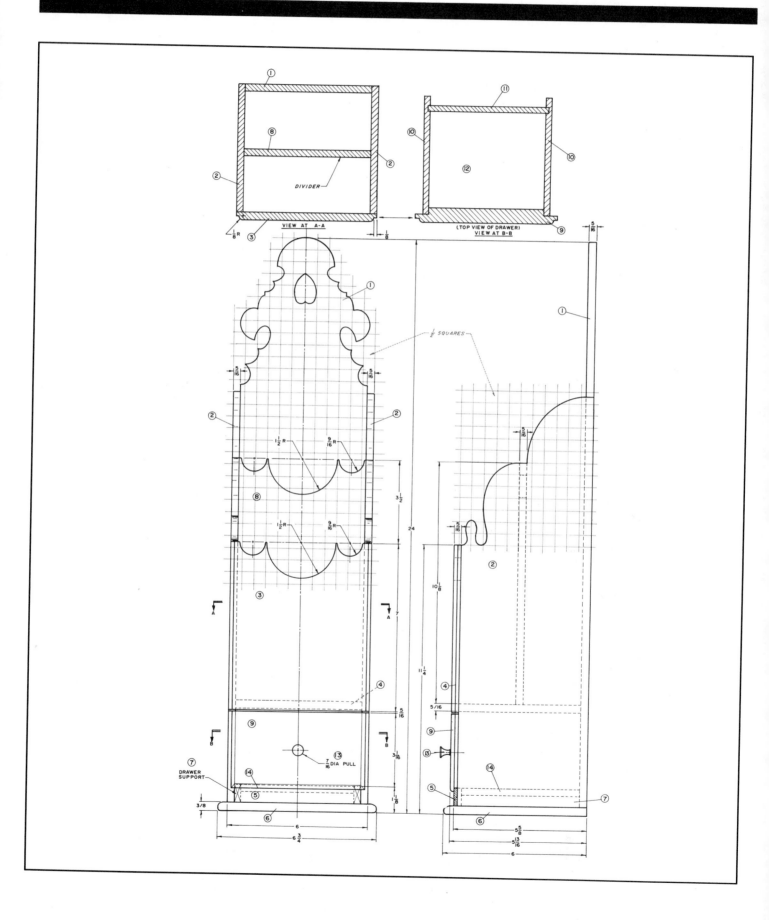

VIEW AT A-A

DIVIDER

(TOP VIEW OF DRAWER)
VIEW AT B-B

½" SQUARES

1½ R   9/16 R

1½ R   9/16 R

DRAWER
SUPPORT

7/16 DIA PULL

24

3½

7

11¼

3/8

6

6¾

3 7/16

1⅛

10⅛

5/16

5⅝

5 13/16

6

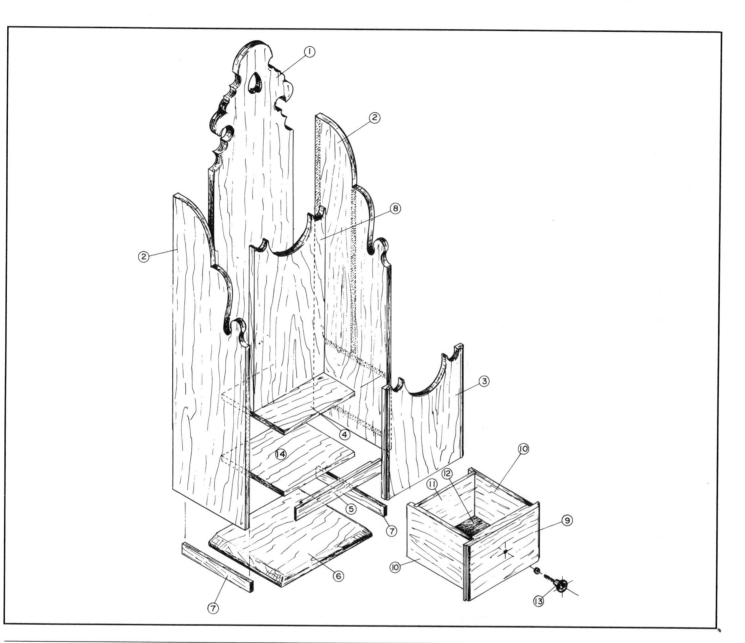

PART		INCHES	NEEDED
1	BACK	$5/16 \times 5^3/8 \times 23^5/8$	1
2	SIDE	$5/16 \times 5^1/2 \times 17^1/8$	2
3	FRONT (1)	$5/16 \times 6 \times 7$	1
4	DIVIDER	$5/16 \times 5^5/16 \times 5^1/8$	1
5	BASE TRIM	$5/16 \times 3/4 \times 5^3/8$	1
6	BASE	$3/8 \times 6 \times 6^3/4$	1
7	SLIDER	$5/16 \times 3/4 \times 5^1/8$	2
8	FRONT (2)	$5/16 \times 6 \times 10$	1
9	DRAWER FRONT	$5/8 \times 3^1/4 \times 6$	1
10	DRAWER SIDE	$1/4 \times 3 \times 5$	2
11	DRAWER BACK	$1/4 \times 3 \times 5$	1
12	DRAWER BOTTOM	$1/4 \times 4^1/4 \times 5$	1
13	BRASS PULL	$7/16$ DIAMETER	1

HANGING WALL SHELVES

Most early wall shelves were made to fit a particular need in a particular room or space. They therefore came in various shapes and sizes. Many had sides with the wavelike cyma curves, as so many early pieces did, perhaps to match other pieces in the room. Some were very plain; others had shelves with dividers. These dividers later developed into drawers. Hanging shelves were built to fit against a wall or in a corner.

Today these wonderful old shelves can be used to display collections and a variety of other objects.

Independence Hall Candleholder

This shelf, a hall candleholder, is modeled after one in Independence Hall in Philadelphia. Use it to display a candlestick and candle. When you light the candle, be sure to remove the top board. This reproduction makes a very formal entrance light. It measures $6^5/8$ inches deep by 11 inches wide by 24 inches tall.

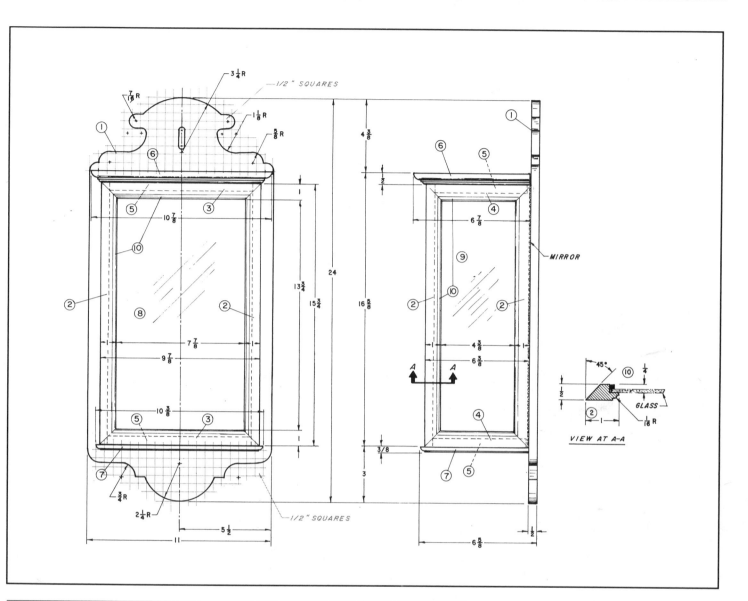

PART		INCHES	NEEDED
1	BACK BOARD	$1/2 \times 11 \times 24$	1
2	STILE	$1/2 \times 1 \times 15^{3}/4$	6
3	RAIL FRONT	$1/2 \times 1 \times 9^{7}/8$	2
4	RAIL SIDE	$1/2 \times 1 \times 6^{3}/4$	4
5	SPACER	$1/4 \times 5^{7}/8 \times 8^{7}/8$	2
6	TOP BOARD	$1/2 \times 6^{7}/8 \times 10^{7}/8$	1
7	BOTTOM BOARD	$3/8 \times 6^{5}/8 \times 10^{3}/8$	1
8	GLASS FRONT	$8^{1}/4 \times 14^{1}/4$	1
9	GLASS SIDE	$4^{7}/8 \times 14^{1}/4$	2
10	GLASS STAY	$1/8 \times 1/8$, 10 FEET	1
11	MIRROR GLASS	CUT TO SIZE	1

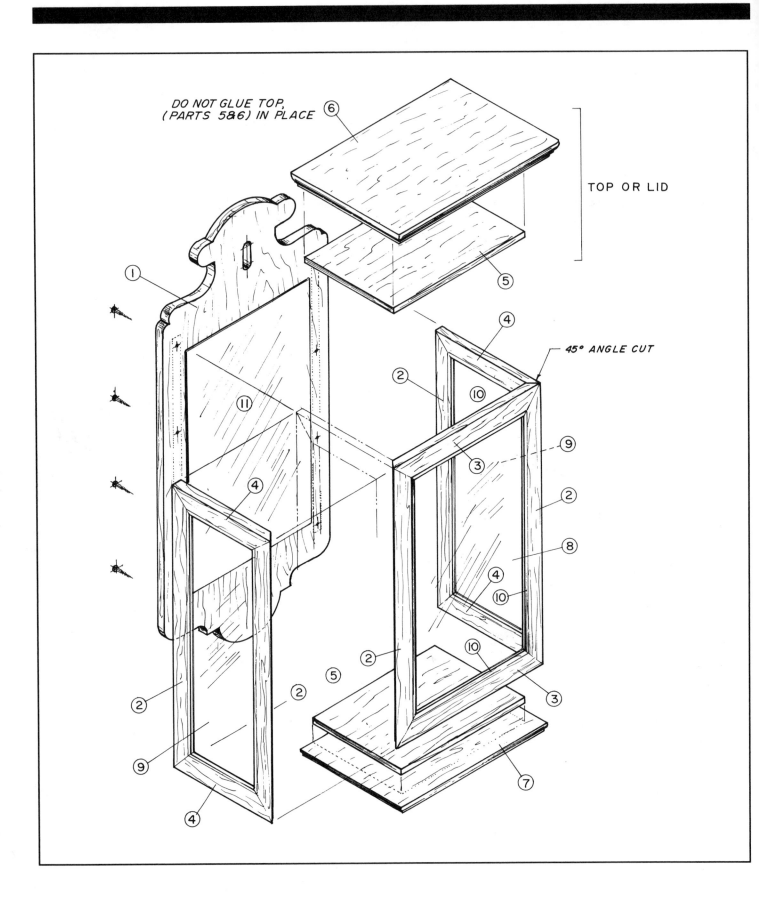

DO NOT GLUE TOP,
(PARTS 5&6) IN PLACE

TOP OR LID

45° ANGLE CUT

Hanging Shelf with Door

The original of this unusual wall shelf, with its wooden hinges and wooden latch, was found in Peterborough, New Hampshire. Although in poor condition, its price was high. It was made of pine, and most of the blue paint was worn away. A mirror 8 by 16 inches could be added inside the door to make the shelf more functional in today's house. This reproduction will add a touch of country, however it is used and wherever it is hung. Dimensions are 4³/₄ inches deep, exclusive of the hardware, 12 inches wide, and 25 inches tall.

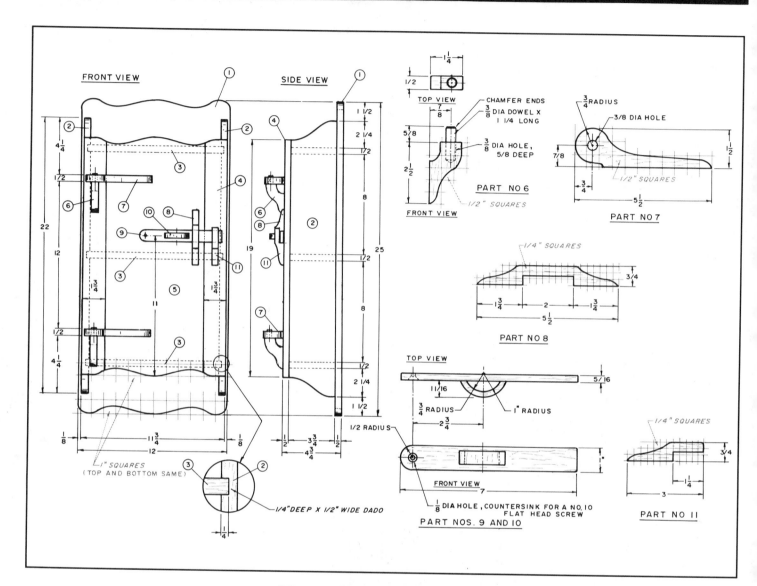

FRONT VIEW

SIDE VIEW

CHAMFER ENDS
3/8 DIA DOWEL X 1 1/4 LONG
3/8 DIA HOLE, 5/8 DEEP

TOP VIEW

FRONT VIEW

PART NO 6

3/4 RADIUS
3/8 DIA HOLE
1/2" SQUARES

PART NO 7

1/4" SQUARES

PART NO 8

TOP VIEW

3/4 RADIUS
1" RADIUS

FRONT VIEW

1/8 DIA HOLE, COUNTERSINK FOR A NO. 10 FLAT HEAD SCREW

PART NOS. 9 AND 10

1/4" SQUARES

PART NO 11

1" SQUARES
(TOP AND BOTTOM SAME)

1/4" DEEP X 1/2" WIDE DADO

1/2 RADIUS

PART	INCHES	NEEDED
1	$1/2 \times 12 \times 25$	1
2	$1/2 \times 3^3/4 \times 22$	2
3	$1/2 \times 3^3/4 \times 11^1/4$	3
4	$1/2 \times 1^3/4 \times 19$	2
5	$1/2 \times 8^1/4 \times 17$	1
6	$1/2 \times 1^1/4 \times 2^1/2$	2
7	$1/2 \times 1^1/2 \times 5^1/2$	2
8	$1/2 \times 3/4 \times 5^1/2$	1
9	$5/16 \times 1 \times 7$	1
10	$1/2 \times 11/16 \times 2$	1
11	$1/2 \times 3/4 \times 3$	1
OTHER MATERIALS:		
1 1/4" LONG, 3/8" DIAMETER DOWEL		2
NO. 10 FLATHEAD WOOD SCREW		1
1 1/2" LONG SQUARE-HEAD NAIL		36

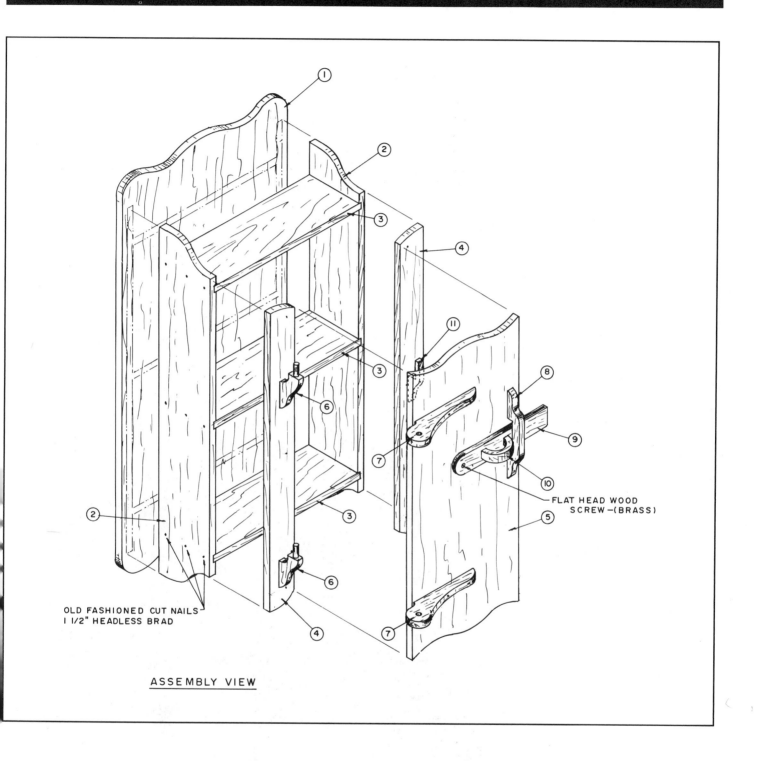

OLD FASHIONED CUT NAILS
1 1/2" HEADLESS BRAD

FLAT HEAD WOOD
SCREW—(BRASS)

ASSEMBLY VIEW

189

Small Corner Shelf

This corner wall shelf was found at a flea market in northern Vermont. Its age is questionable—it may not be an antique—but its lines are pleasing, and so it has been included in this book. Besides, it will become a genuine antique within the next seventy-five years! It measures 9³/₈ inches deep by 20 inches high.

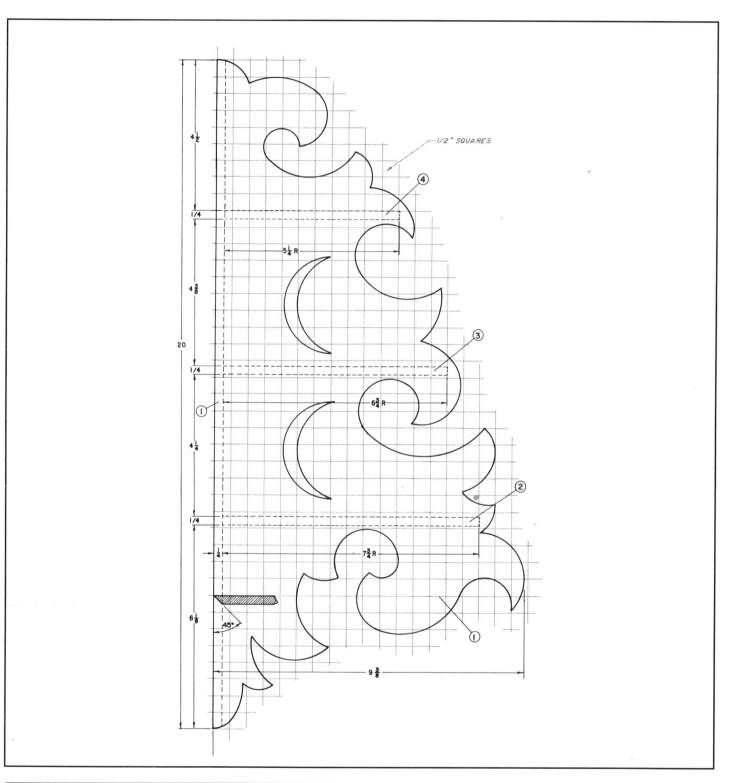

PART		INCHES	NEEDED
1	SIDE	1/4 × 9³/8 × 20	2
2	BOTTOM SHELF	1/4 × 7³/4 SQUARE	1
3	MIDDLE SHELF	1/4 × 6³/4 SQUARE	1
4	TOP SHELF	1/4 × 5¹/4 SQUARE	1

191

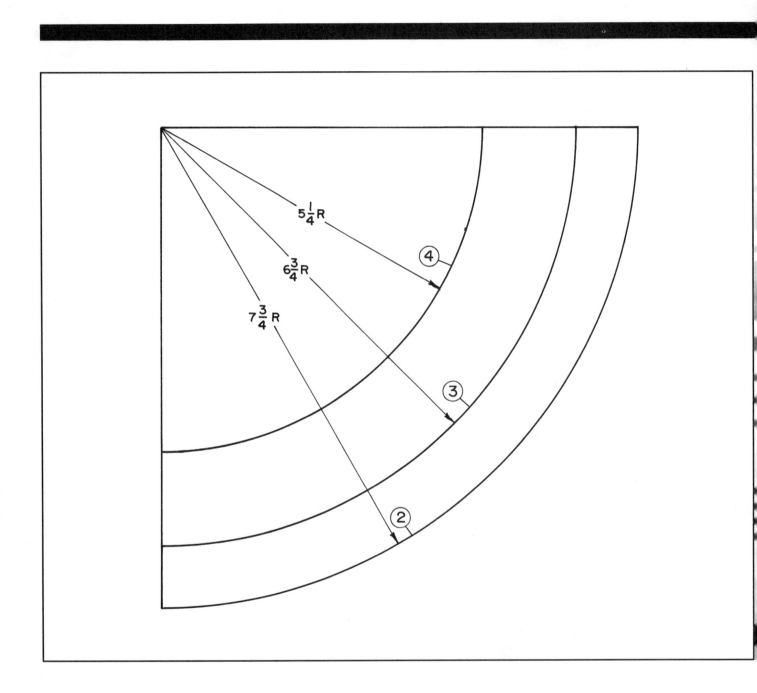

Early Corner Shelf

An early design, the original of this shelf was made of pine. Its origin is unknown. Dimensions are 9⅝ inches deep by 27 inches high.

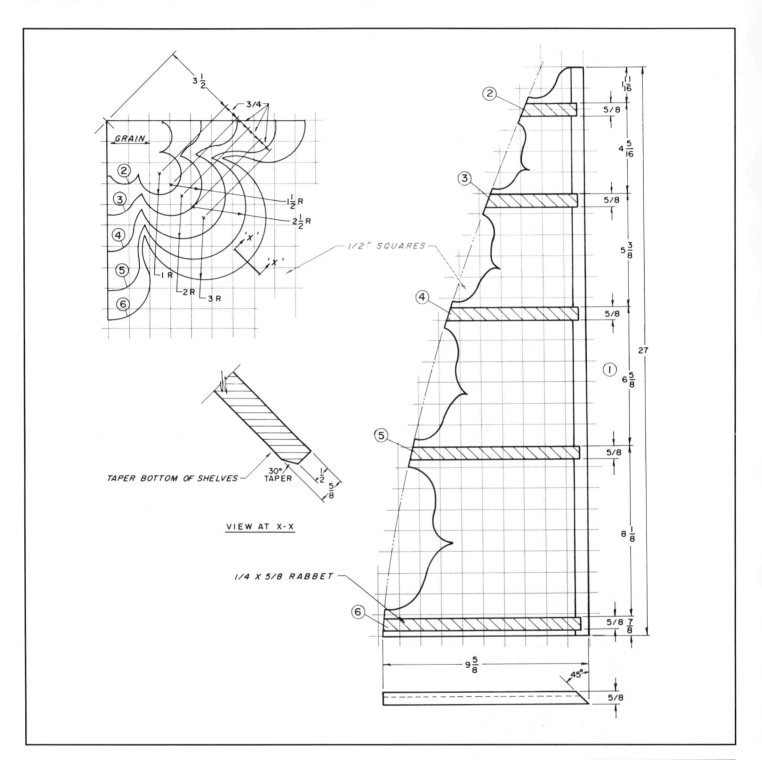

VIEW AT X-X

TAPER BOTTOM OF SHELVES   30° TAPER

GRAIN

1/2" SQUARES

1/4 X 5/8 RABBET

PART		INCHES	NEEDED
1	BODY	⅝ × 9⅝ × 27	2
2	SHELF	⅝ × 4 SQUARE	1
3	SHELF	⅝ × 4½ SQUARE	1
4	SHELF	⅝ × 6½ SQUARE	1
5	SHELF	⅝ × 8½ SQUARE	1
6	SHELF	⅝ × 10 SQUARE	1

Whale Shelf

The original shelf, made around 1840, was painted brown; both it and the reproduction feature simulated wood grain, an effect achieved with black smoke from a candle (see page 24 for instructions on this technique). Its measurements are 9 inches deep by 24 inches wide by 36 inches high.

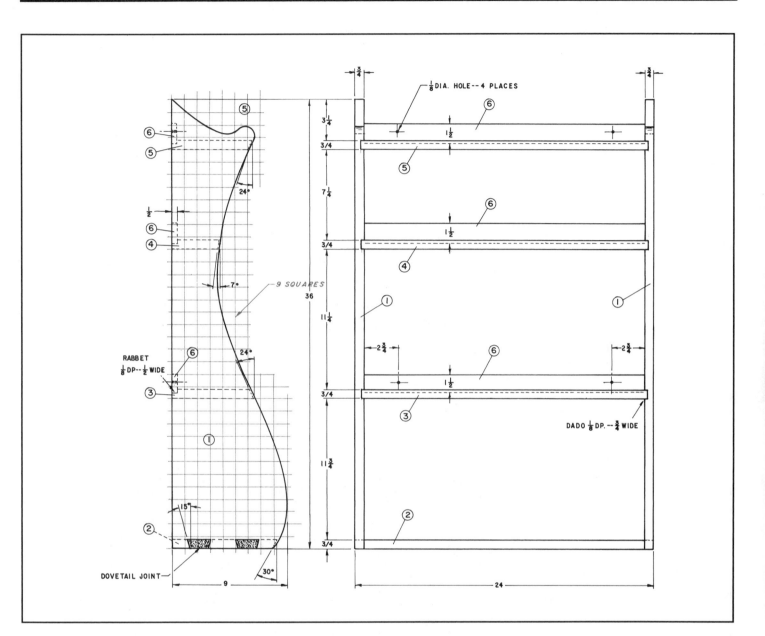

PART	INCHES	NEEDED
1 SIDE	3/4 × 9 × 36	2
2 SHELF	3/4 × 8 1/4 × 24	1
3 SHELF	3/4 × 6 1/2 × 23	1
4 SHELF	3/4 × 3 3/4 × 23	1
5 SHELF	3/4 × 6 1/2 × 23	1
6 BRACE	1/2 × 1 1/2 × 23 1/2	3

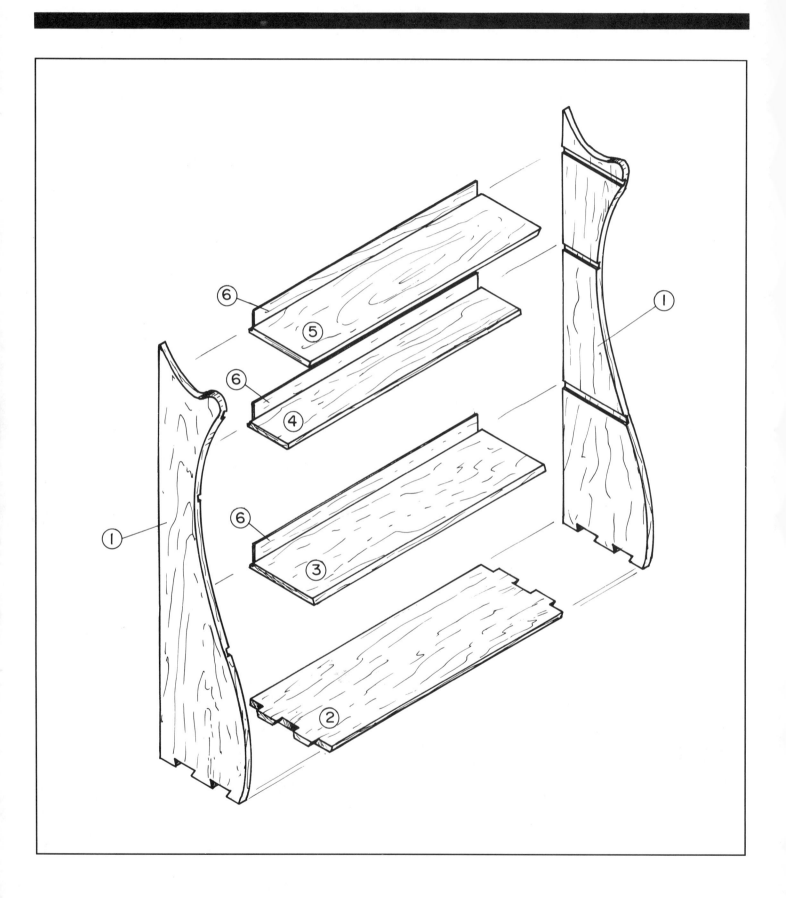

Two-Drawer Shelf

This hanging wall shelf is made of pine; its square-cut nails are left showing. Dimensions are 9 inches deep by 33 inches wide by 41 inches high.

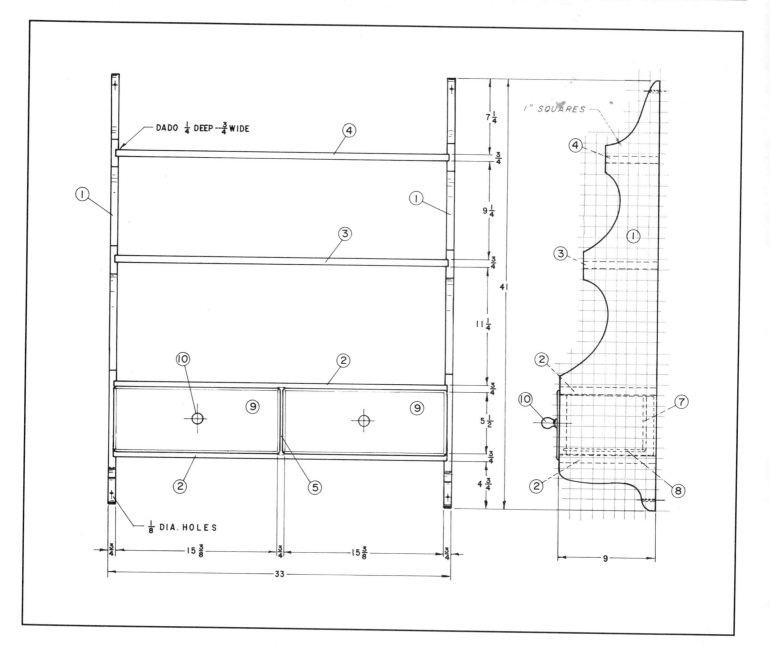

PART		INCHES	NEEDED
1	SIDE	$3/4 \times 9 \times 41$	2
2	SHELF	$3/4 \times 9 \times 32$	2
3	SHELF	$3/4 \times 7 \times 32$	1
4	SHELF	$3/4 \times 5 \times 32$	1
5	DIVIDER	$3/4 \times 9 \times 6$	1
6	DRAWER SIDE	$3/8 \times 5^{1}/2 \times 8^{3}/4$	4
7	DRAWER BACK	$3/8 \times 5^{1}/2 \times 15$	2
8	DRAWER BOTTOM	$1/4 \times 8^{1}/2 \times 15$	2
9	DRAWER FRONT	$5/8 \times 6 \times 15^{5}/8$	2
10	WOODEN DRAWER PULL	$3/4$ DIAMETER	2

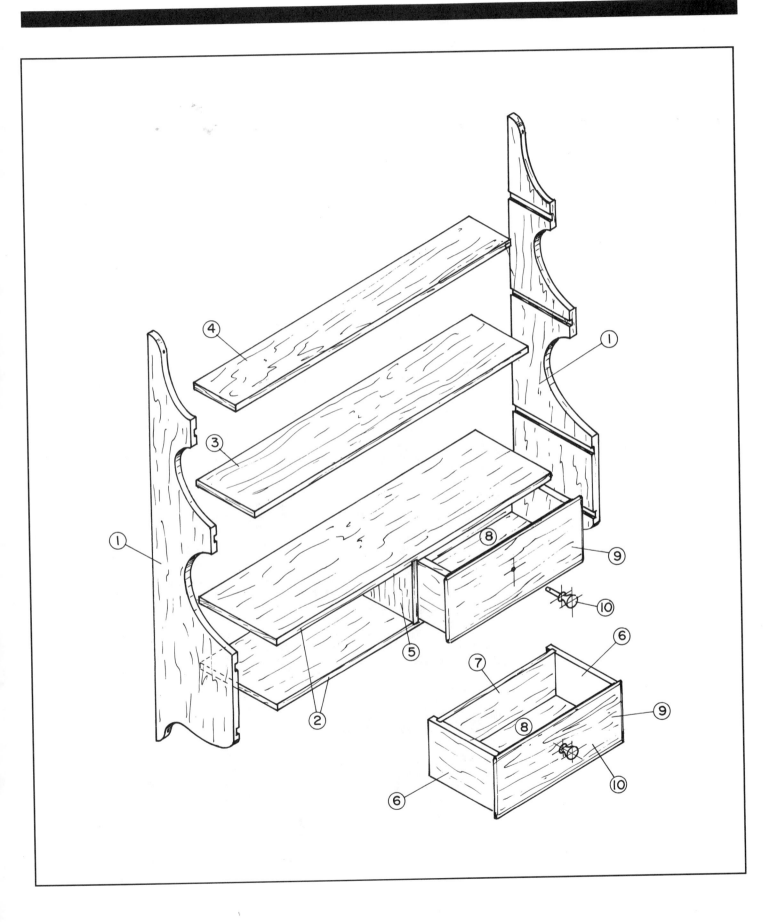

Country Wall Shelf

Constructed with dovetail joints, this shelf has cyma-curved sides. The original, from Pennsylvania, was made of pine and painted red; it dates to 1825. Measurements are 5½ inches deep plus the top molding, 29 inches wide, and 35 inches high.

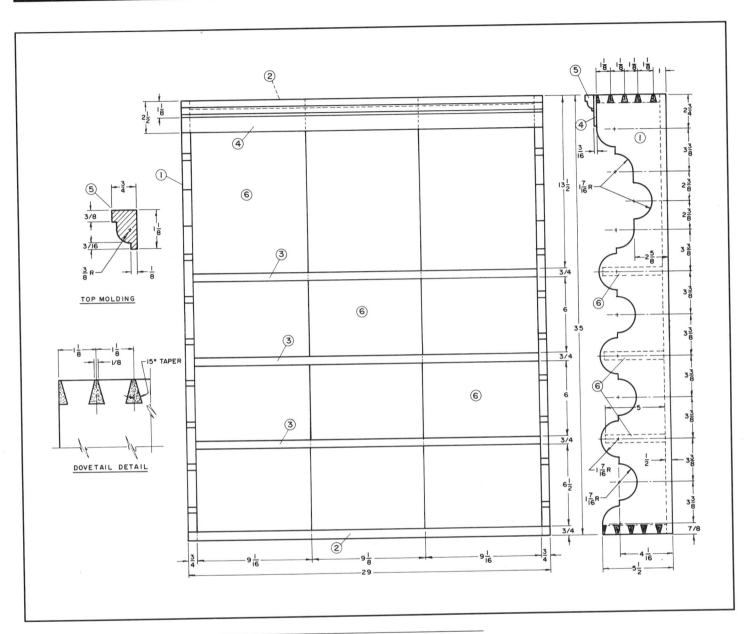

TOP MOLDING

15° TAPER

DOVETAIL DETAIL

PART	INCHES	NEEDED
1 SIDE	$3/4 \times 5^{1}/_{2} \times 35$	2
2 TOP / BOTTOM	$3/4 \times 5 \times 29$	2
3 SHELF	$3/4 \times 4^{3}/_{4} \times 27^{1}/_{4}$	3
4 RAIL	$3/16 \times 2^{1}/_{2} \times 29$	1
5 MOLDING	$3/4 \times 1^{1}/_{8} \times 29$	1
6 BACK	$1/2 \times 9^{1}/_{8} \times 35$	3

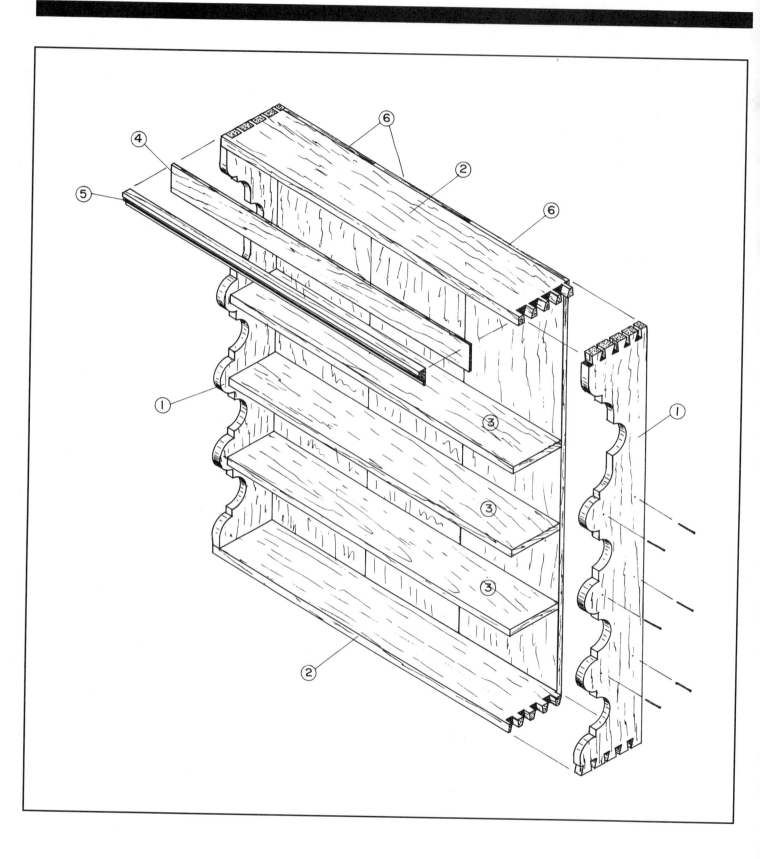

Elegant Wall Shelf

The original of this wall shelf was found in Peterborough, New Hampshire, in an antique shop. The graceful, stepped cyma sides and the large top make this set of shelves unusual. It was made around 1840, of pine (the copy is made of cherry). Its dimensions are 9 inches deep by 25½ inches wide by 32½ inches high.

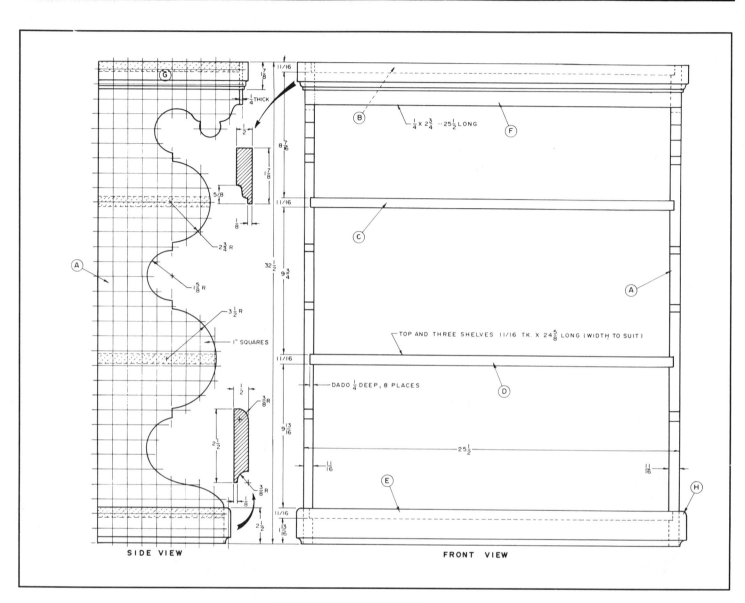

SIDE VIEW

FRONT VIEW

PART	INCHES	NEEDED
A SIDE	$^{11}/_{16}$ × 10 × 32$^1/_2$	2
B TOP BOARD	$^{11}/_{16}$ × 10 × 24$^5/_8$	1
C TOP SHELF	$^{11}/_{16}$ × 8 × 24$^5/_8$	1
D MIDDLE SHELF	$^{11}/_{16}$ × 8$^1/_4$ × 24$^5/_8$	1
E BOTTOM SHELF	$^{11}/_{16}$ × 8$^3/_4$ × 24$^5/_8$	1
F FRONT	$^1/_4$ × 2$^3/_4$ × 25$^1/_2$	1
G TOP MOLDING	$^1/_2$ × 1$^7/_8$ × 48	1
H BASE MOLDING	$^1/_2$ × 2$^1/_2$ × 48	1

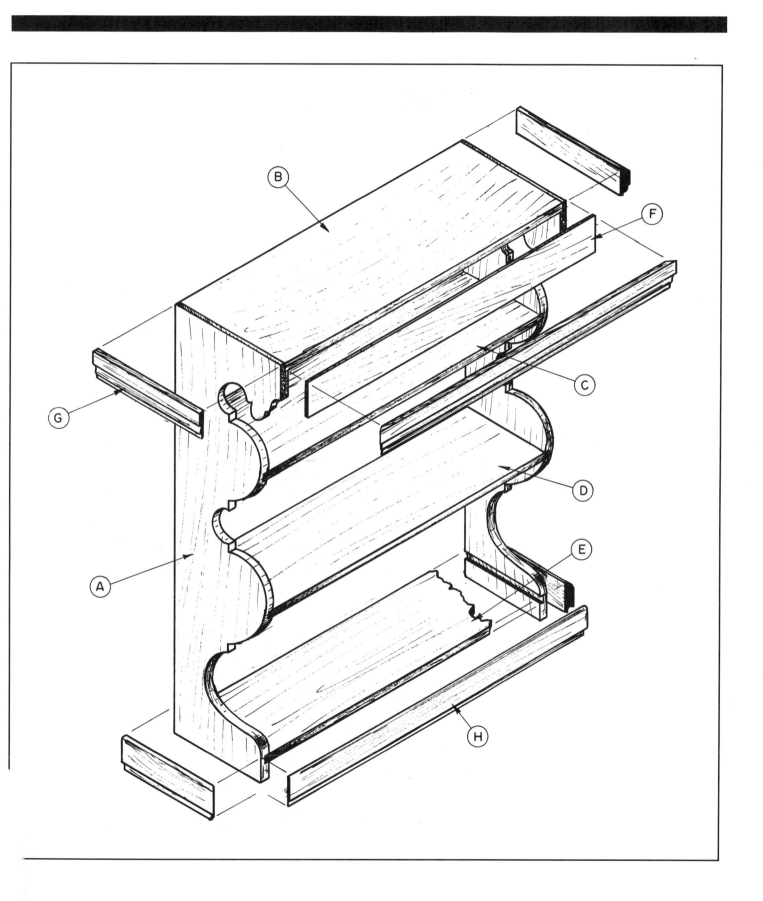

Primitive Shelf

This shelf has iron butterfly hinges and an escutcheon plate. The original was made around 1725 and painted powder blue. It is of butternut except for the drawer, which is of pine. It comes from Pennsylvania. Dimensions are 8 inches deep plus the molding, 15½ inches wide, and 26 inches high.

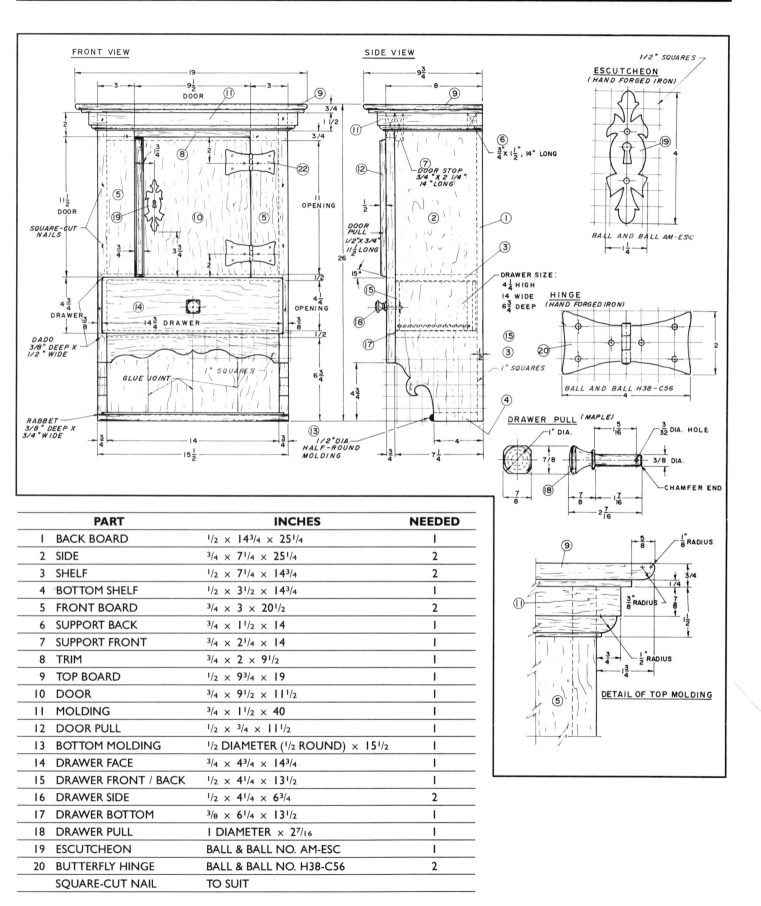

FRONT VIEW

SIDE VIEW

ESCUTCHEON
(HAND FORGED IRON)

1/2" SQUARES

BALL AND BALL AM-ESC

HINGE
(HAND FORGED IRON)

BALL AND BALL H38-C56

DRAWER PULL (MAPLE)

DETAIL OF TOP MOLDING

PART		INCHES	NEEDED
1	BACK BOARD	1/2 × 14³/4 × 25¹/4	1
2	SIDE	3/4 × 7¹/4 × 25¹/4	2
3	SHELF	1/2 × 7¹/4 × 14³/4	2
4	BOTTOM SHELF	1/2 × 3¹/2 × 14³/4	1
5	FRONT BOARD	3/4 × 3 × 20¹/2	2
6	SUPPORT BACK	3/4 × 1¹/2 × 14	1
7	SUPPORT FRONT	3/4 × 2¹/4 × 14	1
8	TRIM	3/4 × 2 × 9¹/2	1
9	TOP BOARD	1/2 × 9³/4 × 19	1
10	DOOR	3/4 × 9¹/2 × 11¹/2	1
11	MOLDING	3/4 × 1¹/2 × 40	1
12	DOOR PULL	1/2 × 3/4 × 11¹/2	1
13	BOTTOM MOLDING	1/2 DIAMETER (1/2 ROUND) × 15¹/2	1
14	DRAWER FACE	3/4 × 4³/4 × 14³/4	1
15	DRAWER FRONT / BACK	1/2 × 4¹/4 × 13¹/2	1
16	DRAWER SIDE	1/2 × 4¹/4 × 6³/4	2
17	DRAWER BOTTOM	3/8 × 6¹/4 × 13¹/2	1
18	DRAWER PULL	1 DIAMETER × 2⁷/16	1
19	ESCUTCHEON	BALL & BALL NO. AM-ESC	1
20	BUTTERFLY HINGE	BALL & BALL NO. H38-C56	2
	SQUARE-CUT NAIL	TO SUIT	

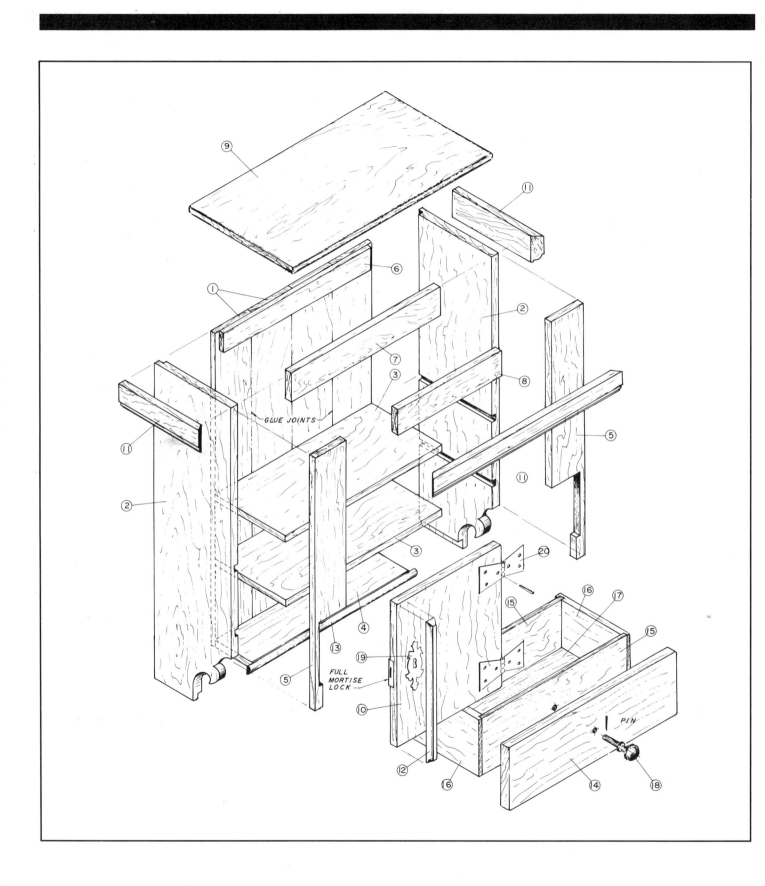

TABLE

The half-round table was a favorite variation on the rectangular and square tables made by the colonists and early Americans. Most half-round tables had three legs, but some had four. The design of these early tables usually included an apron. They make wonderful tables for the hall, where space is limited.

Half-Round Table

Of pine, the original of this table was made around 1850. Its origin is unknown. Note that the legs do not taper in this slightly awkward but original design. The table stands 26 inches high; it is 18 inches deep and 36 inches wide.

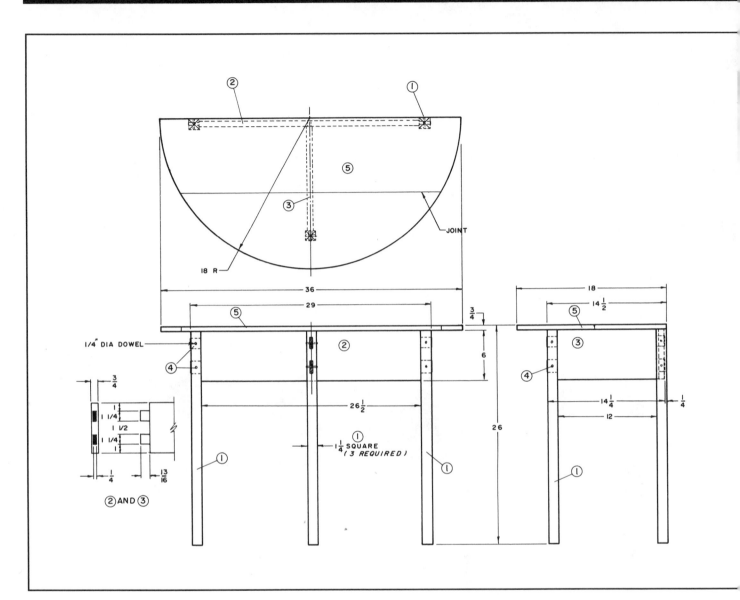

PART	INCHES	NEEDED
1 LEG	1¼ SQUARE × 25¼	3
2 MAIN RAIL	¾ × 6 × 29	1
3 RAIL	¾ × 6 × 14½	1
4 PIN	¼ DIAMETER × 1¼	6
5 TOP	¾ × 18 × 36	1
6 BLOCK	¾ × ¾ × 2	3

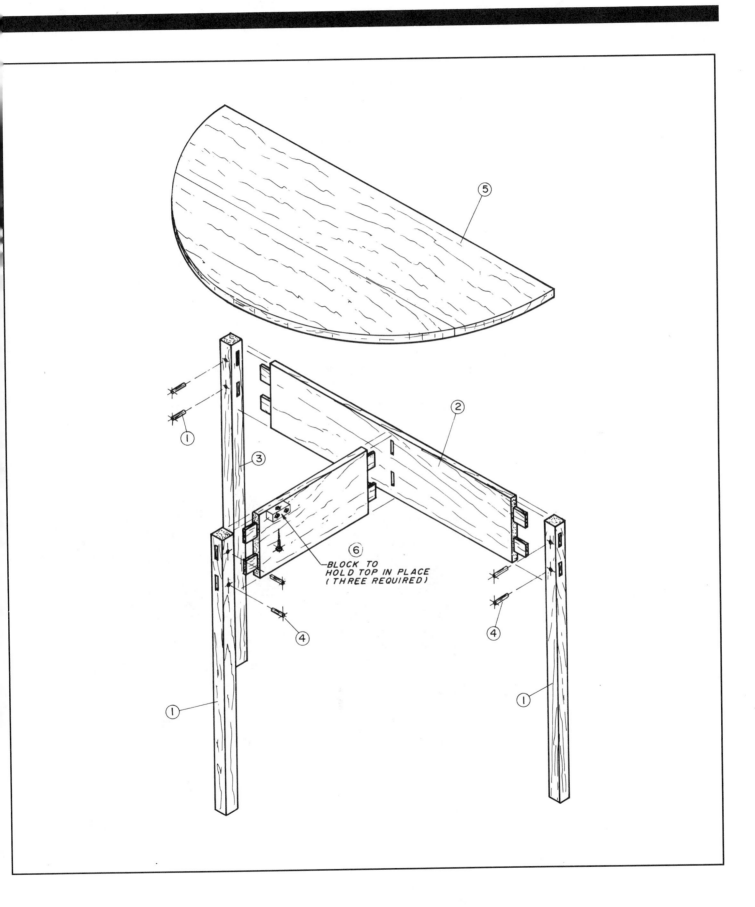

BLOCK TO
HOLD TOP IN PLACE
(THREE REQUIRED)

BLANKET CHEST

Ships' records indicate that the chest was the only item accompanying most early settlers on their voyage to the New World—perhaps it was originally used as a suitcase. Once they had arrived, the chest continued to be an important article: Early homes had no closets in which people could store their clothes and blankets, attics were not readily accessible, and cellars were often too damp. Thus, the blanket chest remained popular from the 1700s through 1850 or so.

 Blanket chests were simply large, six-board boxes with hinged lids. They doubled as places to sit in the very early homes, where furniture was scarce. Many were painted and decorated with folk art.

 The project that follows is a small blanket chest that can find many uses in today's homes.

Child's Blanket Chest

This is an unusually small blanket chest—a miniature, really—and of a nice size for today's living. The original was made of pine, painted salmon. The snipe hinges are a sure sign that it is very old. This little chest measures 12 inches deep by 21½ inches wide by 20 inches high.

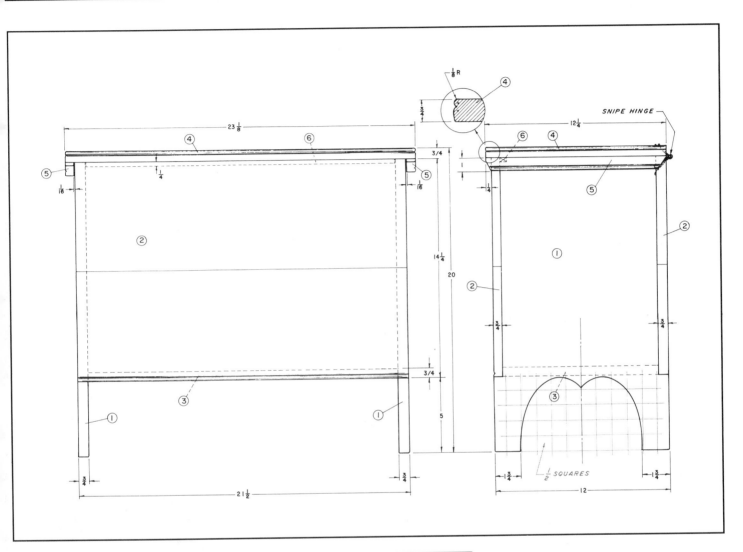

PART	INCHES	NEEDED
1 END	³/₄ × 12 × 19¹/₄	2
2 FRONT / BACK	³/₄ × 14¹/₄ × 21¹/₂	2
3 BOTTOM	³/₄ × 10¹/₂ × 20	1
4 TOP BOARD	³/₄ × 12¹/₄ × 23¹/₈	1
5 BATTEN	³/₄ × 1 × 12¹/₄	2
6 DUST STOP	¹/₄ × ³/₄ × 19⁷/₈	1

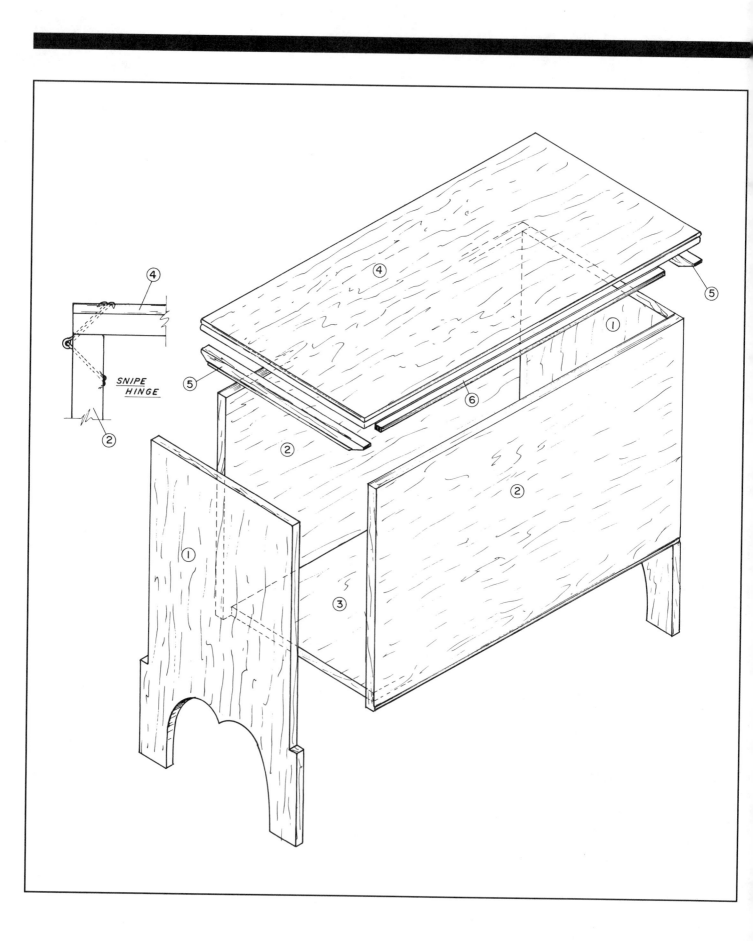

SNIPE
HINGE

Appendices

SUPPLIERS

BEVELED GLASS

Beveled Glass Works
11721 S.E. Talor
Portland, OR 97216

MEASURED DRAWINGS OF ANTIQUES

Caryle Lynch
196 Holly Hill
Broadway, VA 22815

John A. Nelson
220 General Miller Rd.
Peterborough, NH 03458

PAINT

Cohasset Colonials
Cohasset, MA 02025

Stulb Paint and Chemical Co., Inc.
P.O. Box 297
Norristown, PA 19404

MILK PAINT

The Old-Fashioned Milk Paint Co.
Main St.
Groton, MA 01450

Stulb Paint and Chemical Co., Inc.
P.O. Box 297
Norristown, PA 19404

STAINS, TUNG OIL

Cohasset Colonials
Cohasset, MA 02025

Deft, Inc.
17451 Von Darman Ave.
Irvine, CA 92713

Formby's, Inc.
825 Crossover Lane, Ste. 240
Memphis, TN 38117

Stulb Paint and Chemical Co., Inc.
P.O. Box 297
Norristown, PA 19404

Watco-Dennis Corp.
Michigan Ave. and 22nd St.
Santa Monica, CA 90404

OLD-FASHIONED NAILS, BRASS SCREWS

DRI Industries
11300 Hampshire Ave. S.
Bloomington, MN 55438

Equality Screw Co., Inc.
P.O. Box 1296
El Cajon, CA 92002

Horton Brasses
P.O. Box 95
Nooks Hill Rd.
Cromwell, CT 06416

Tremont Nail Co.
P.O. Box 111
21 Elm St.
Wareham, MA 02571

BRASSES

Anglo-American Brass Co.
P.O. Box 9792
4146 Mitzi Dr.
San Jose, CA 95157

Ball and Ball
463 W. Lincoln Hwy.
Exton, PA 19341

The Brass Tree
308 N. Main St.
Charles, MO 63301

Garrett Wade Co., Inc.
161 Avenue of the Americas
New York, NY 10013

Heirloom Antiques Brass Co.
P.O. Box 146
Dundass, MN 55019

Horton Brasses
P.O. Box 95
Nooks Hill Rd.
Cromwell, CT 06416

Imported European Hardware
4295 S. Arville
Las Vegas, NV 89103

Mason and Sullivan Co.
586 Higgins Crowell Rd.
West Yarmouth, MA 02678

19th Century Hardware Supply Co.
P.O. Box 599
Rough and Ready, CA 95975

The Renovators' Supply
The Old Mill
Millers Falls, MA 01349

The Shop, Inc.
P.O. Box 3711, R.D. 3
Reading, PA 19606

Ritter and Son Hardware
Dept. WJ
Gualala, CA 95445

FINE WOOD

CraftWoods
10921 York Rd.
Cockeysville, MD 21030

Hardwoods of Memphis
P.O. Box 12449
Memphis, TN 38182

Manny's Woodworking Pl.
602 S. Broadway
Lexington, KY 40508

Woodcrafters of Spring Green Wisconsin
P.O. Box 566
Spring Green, WI 53588

Woods of the World, Inc.
P.O. Box 112
Rt. 202
Antrim, NH 03440
(Largest wood supplier in the Northeast.)

VENEERING

Bob Morgan Woodworking Supplies
1123 Bardstown Rd.
Louisville, KY 40204

GENERAL CATALOGS

Brookstone Co.
Vose Farm Rd.
Peterborough, NH 03458

Constantine
2050 Eastchester Rd.
Bronx, NY 10461

Cryder Creek Wood Shoppe, Inc.
P.O. Box 19
Whitesville, NY 14897

The Fine Tool Shops
P.O. Box 1262
20 Backus Ave.
Danbury, CT 06810

Garrettwade
161 Ave. of the Americas
New York, NY 10013

Leichtung, Inc.
4944 Commerce Pkwy.
Cleveland, OH 44128

Silvo Hardware Co.
2205 Richmond St.
Philadelphia, PA 19125

Trendlines
375 Beacham St.
Chelsea, MA 02150

Woodcraft Supply
P.O. Box 4000
41 Atlantic Ave.
Woburn, MA 01888

The Woodworkers Store
21801 Industrial Blvd.
Rogers, MN 55374

Woodworkers Supply of New Mexico
5604 Alameda, N.E.
Albuquerque, NM 87113

CLOCK SUPPLIES

H. DeCounick & Son
P.O. Box 68
200 Market Plaza
Alamo, CA 94507

S. LaRose, Inc.
234 Commerce Pl.
Greensboro, NC 27420

Mason and Sullivan Co.
586 Higgins Crowell Rd.
West Yarmouth, MA 02678

Merritt's Antiques, Inc.
Rt. 2
Douglassville, PA 19518

STENCILING SUPPLIES

Adelle Bishop, Inc.
Dorset, VT 05251

Creative Arts & Crafts, Inc.
P.O. Box 11491
Knoxville, TN 37939-1491

RELATED PUBLICATIONS

American Woodworker
33 E. Minor St.
Emmaus, PA 18098

Early American Life
P.O. Box 8200
Harrisburg, PA 17105

Fine Woodworking
The Taunton Press
P.O. Box 355
52 Church Hill Rd.
Newton, CT 06470

International Woodworking Magazine
Plymouth, NH 03264

Popular Woodworker
EGW Publishing Co.
1300 Galaxy Way
Concord, CA 94520

Wood
P.O. Box 10625
Des Moines, IA 50380-0625

Woodsmith
2200 Grand Ave.
Des Moines, IA 50312

The Woodworkers Journal
P.O. Box 1629
517 Litchfield Rd.
New Milford, CT 06776

Workbench Magazine
P.O. Box 5965
Kansas City, MO 64110

WOODWORKING ASSOCIATIONS, CLUBS, AND GUILDS

Alabama Woodworkers Guild
P.O. Box 327
Pelham, AL 35214

Alaska Creative Woodworkers
Greg Motyka
2136 Alder Dr.
Anchorage, AK 99508

Augusta Woodworkers Guild
P.O. Box 15
Augusta, MO 63332

Baulines Craftsman Guild
55 Sunnyside
Mill Valley, CA 94941

Green Country Woodworkers Club
P.O. Box 470856
Tulsa, OK 74147-0856

Guild of Oregon Woodworkers
P.O. Box 1866
Portland, OR 97207

Inland Empire Woodworkers Guild
P.O. Box 7413
Spokane, WA 99207

Kansas City Woodworkers Guild
510 N. Sterling
Sugar Creek, MO 64054

Michigan Woodworkers Guild
P.O. Box 7802
Ann Arbor, MI 48107

Midwest Woodworkers Association
Gerald Jones
311 Cumberland Rd.
Columbia, MO 65203

North Texas Woodworkers Guild
P.O. Box 224886
Dallas, TX 75222

Society of Philadelphia Woodworkers
c/o Chestnut Hill Academy
500 W. Willow Grove Ave.
Philadelphia, PA 19118

Souris Valley Woodworkers Association
P.O. Box 3042
Minot, ND 58702

Southeast American Craft Council
Art Dept.
Longwood College
Farmville, VA 23901

Vancouver Island Woodworkers Guild
Box 6584, Station C
Victoria, British Columbia
Canada V8P 5N7

Virginia Mountain Crafts Guild
P.O. Box 1001
Salem, VA 24153

Wisconsin Woodworkers Guild
Jim Lingle, President
P.O. Box 137
Milwaukee, WI 53201

Woodworkers Association of
North America
P.O. Box 706
Plymouth, NH 03264

Woodworkers Association of Topeka
Cleo McDonald, President
9421 N.W. 42nd St.
Silver Lake, KS 66539

Woodworkers' Guild of Georgia
P.O. Box 1113
Conyers, GA 30207

Woodwrights Gallery
P.O. Box 7571
Klamath Falls, OR 97602

FOR FURTHER STUDY

The following list includes places where antique furniture can be found and studied. It is a good idea first to write any place you wish to visit to find out the visiting hours.

American Clock and Watch Museum
100 Maple St.
Bristol, CT 06010

Bennington Museum
W. Main St.
Bennington, VT 05201

Boston Museum of Fine Arts
465 Huntington Ave.
Boston, MA 02115

Colonial Williamsburg
P.O. Box C
Williamsburg, VA 23187

Farmers' Museum
P.O. Box 800
Lake Road
Cooperstown, NY 13326

Hancock Shaker Village
P.O. Box 898, Rt. 20
Pittsfield, MA 01202

Henry Ford Museum and Greenfield Village
P.O. Box 1970
Dearborn, MI 48121

Index of American Design
6th and Constitution Ave., N.W.
Washington, DC 20565

Landis Valley Farm Museum
Lancaster, PA 17600

Maritime Museum
2905 Hyde St.
San Francisco, CA 94123

Metropolitan Museum of Art
82d St. and 5th Ave.
New York, NY 10028

Mystic Seaport
P.O. Box 6000
Mystic, CT 06355

National Gallery of Art
Washington, DC 20565

Old Deerfield Village
Deerfield, MA 01342

Old Salem
Drawer F
Winston Salem, NC 27108

Old Sturbridge Village
1 Old Sturbridge Village Rd.
Sturbridge, MA 01566-0200

Philadelphia Museum of Art
P.O. Box 7646
Philadelphia, PA 19101-7646

Plimoth Plantation
P.O. Box 1620
Warren Ave.
Plymouth, MA 02360

Salem Harbor
54 Turner St.
Salem, MA 01970

Saugus Iron Works
244 Central St.
Saugus, MA 01906

Shelburne Museum
Rt. 7
Shelburne, VT 05401

Smithsonian Institution
10th and Constitution, N.W.
Washington, DC 20560

Strawberry Banke Museum
P.O. Box 300
454 Court St.
Portsmouth, NH 03801

Thomas Lee House
Old Lyme, CT 06371

Wenham Museum
132 Main St., Rt., 1A
Wenham, MA 01984